Celebrity Chefs of Country Music & Motorsports

ISBN: 0-9634042-0-2

Copyright © 2001
Lehi Christian Children's Foundation
Salem, Virginia

Designed by Multimedia Creations, Inc.

1st Printing   April 2001
Printed in the United States of America

Additional copies may be obtained at the cost of $27.95, US / $38.95 Canada
plus $5.95* postage and handling for each book.
Virginia residents add $1.53 sales tax for each book (4.5%)

* For orders outside continental United States, or multiple books, call for shipping fee.

For your convenience, an order form is included in the back of this book.

Make checks out to:

LEHI CHRISTIAN CHILDREN'S FOUNDATION

Send orders to:

LEHI CHRISTIAN CHILDREN'S FOUNDATION
817 Connecticut Avenue
Roanoke, Virginia 24012

toll free: 1-800-861-7355

website: www.celebritychefs.org
email: sales@celebritychefs.org

Thank You

We at Lehi Christian Children's Foundation would like to express a thank you to all of you that made this beautiful cookbook possible. Without your generous contributions, it couldn't have happened. This is a great expression of love and compassion.

Our ministry is to help the children of America. Many of these children go to bed hungry, do not have suitable clothes to wear to school, or even have warm homes to live in. With your help, we can work to change this. With the proceeds from this book, we promise to reach as many of the needy children in America as we can. There is at present over five million Americans living well below the poverty line in this country. (Source; Brian Williams, NBC) From those that are dependent on soup kitchens daily, four in ten are children. This should not be a fact in America with all the resources we have.

With the purchase of this cookbook, you'll always be a part of this ministry. God said when we reach out to these, we reach Him.

Table of Contents

Appetizers & Beverages 1

Breads & Breakfast 17

Cakes 41

Casseroles 63

Chili 93

Cookies & Desserts 107

Meat 129

Pasta 151

Pies 161

Poultry 173

Salads 201

Sauces & Soups 217

Seafood 233

Vegetables 249

Index of Celebrities 263

Kitchen Measurements

Eggs

Whole	Egg Whites	Egg Yolks
1 medium = 1/4 cup	2 = 1/4 cup	3 = 1/4 cup
2 medium = 1/3 to 1/2 cup	3 = 3/8 cup	4 = 1/3 cup
3 medium = 1/2 to 2/3 cup	4 = 1/2 cup	5 = 3/8 cup
4 medium = 2/3 to 1 cup	5 = 2/3 cup	6 = 1/2 cup

Butter

For approximate measure:

4 sticks (1 lb.) = 2 cups
1 stick (1/4 lb.) = 1/2 cup
1/2 stick (1/8 lb.) = 1/4 cup

Most Commonly Used Nuts

	Nuts in Shell	Shelled Nuts
Almonds	1 lb. = 1 to 1-3/4 cups nutmeats	1 lb. = 3-1/2 cups nutmeats
Peanuts	1 lb. = 2-1/4 cups nutmeats	1 lb. = 3 cups nutmeats
Pecans	1 lb. = 2-1/4 cups nutmeats	1 lb. = 4 cups nutmeats
Walnuts	1 lb. = 1-2/3 cups nutmeats	1 lb. = 4 cups nutmeats

Emergency Substitutions

For	Use
1 tbsp. cornstarch (for thickening)	2 tbsp. flour (approximately)
1 whole egg	2 egg yolks plus 1 tbsp. water (in cookies)
1 whole egg	2 egg yolks (in custards & puddings)
1 cup fresh whole milk	1/2 cup evaporated milk plus 1/2 cup water
1 cup fresh whole milk	1 cup reconstituted nonfat dry milk plus 2 tbsp. butter
1 cup fresh whole milk	1 cup sour milk or buttermilk plus 1/2 tsp. soda (decrease baking powder 2 tsp.)
1 cup sour milk or buttermilk	1 tbsp. lemon juice or vinegar plus enough fresh whole milk to make 1 cup
1 sq. unsweetened chocolate (1 oz.)	3 tbsp. cocoa plus 1 tbsp. fat
1 cup honey	1-1/4 cups sugar plus 1/4 cup liquid
1 cup canned tomatoes	about 1-1/3 cups cut-up fresh tomatoes, simmered 10 minutes

Abbreviations

lb. = pound	qt. = quart		
oz. = ounce	tsp. = teaspoon		
pkg. = package	tbsp. = tablespoon		
pt. = pint	sq. = square		

Simplified Measures

dash = less than 1/8 tsp.	2 cups = 1 pint
3 tsp. = 1 tbsp.	2 pints (4 cups) = 1 quart
16 tbsp. = 1 cup	4 quarts (liquid) = 1 gallon
1 cup = 1/2 pint	16 ounces = 1 pound

Appetizers
&
Beverages

Appetizers & Beverages

Amanda's Sausage Balls 3

Artichoke Dip 4

Buffy's Cracker Spread 5

Calamari Fritti 6

Chipped Beef Dip 7

Hilda Stuart's Tea Punch 8

Hot Cheese Dip 9

Lowfat Fruit Drink 10

Michael Waltrip's Favorite Meat and Cheese Hors d'oeuvres 11

Orange Tea 12

Santa's Eggnog 13

Stuffed Bacon Rolls 14

Taco Dip 15

Appetizers & Beverages

Amanda Thomas

Amanda's Sausage Balls

1 roll Jimmy Dean Hot
   Sausage
1 medium package Sergeants
   Cheddar Cheese (lowfat or
   regular)
1 large can Hungry Jack
   Instant Biscuits

Place biscuit dough, cheese and sausage into a medium size mixing bowl and combine ingredients until well blended. Shape mixture with hands into balls or spoon onto a cookie sheet sprayed lightly with Pam. Place cookie sheet into a pre-heated 400 degree oven for 10-15 minutes.

Serve as an appetizer, snack or as a breakfast food.

Lorrie Morgan

Artichoke Dip

1 can artichokes (mashed)
1 cup Parmasean cheese (Kraft)
1/2 cup Kraft mayonnaise

Mix and heat in oven until bubbly hot. Eat with chips or crackers.

Born June 27, Lorrie grew up the daughter of Grand Ole Opry star George Morgan. She spent many nights backstage at the Opry, and made her debut there at age 13. Her father died when she was 16, and she was singing professionally a year later. Her career took off in 1989 with the release of "Dear Me". Lorrie Morgan's career continues to grow.

Buffy's Cracker Spread

1 can small shrimp, chopped
1 (8 oz.) pkg. cream cheese, soft
2 tbls. lemon juice
3 green onions, minced
2 tbls. mayonnaise
1 tbls. worchestershire sauce
Salt and pepper to taste

Michael Waltrip

Combine all ingredients, serve with crackers.

Born April 30, Michael resides in Sherrills Ford, North Carolina. He lives with his wife, Buffy, and their two children, Caitlin Marie and Macy. Michael has been dreaming of racing since the age of 11 when he climbed into a Go Cart, deciding then his profession would be race car driving. He dreamed that one day he would be like his brother, Darrell, and winning races.

Troy Beebe

Calamari Fritti

2 lbs. small, fresh squid
1 1/2 cups flour
1 1/2 tsp. coarse salt
1 tsp. freshly ground black pepper
Oil, for deep-frying (1 part olive oil, 3
    parts vegetable oil)
Lemon wedges

Clean squid, remove tentacles, and cut bodies into 1/4 inch rings. Combine flour, salt, and pepper in bag. Dredge squid rings and tentacles in flour, shaking off excess. Transfer floured squid to a plate.

Heat about 3 inches of oil in a wok or deep-fryer to 375 degrees F. Use a thermometer to check the oil temperature and to maintain it during frying. Fry squid in batches until golden and crisp, about 1 minute. Transfer with a slotted spoon to a warm baking sheet lined with paper towels. Keep warm in a low oven while you fry the remaining batches. Pile fried squid on a serving platter and surround with lemon wedges.

Serves 4 as an appetizer.

Ward Burton

Chipped Beef Dip

8 oz. cream cheese softened
2 tsp. milk
1 jar chipped beef
1 tsp. minced onion
1/8 tsp. pepper
2 tsp. chopped green pepper
1/2 cup sour cream

Combine cream cheese and milk. Then add remaining ingredients. Put in oven safe bowl and bake at 350 for 15 minutes. Serve with crackers or rye bread.

This is a recipe of Ward's grandmother, and has always been one of his favorites. Ward has been racing since he was 8 and raced Go Karts and he worked his way up racing Street Stocks, and then racing in the Busch Series. Ward resides in South Boston, Virginia and lives with his wife, Tabatha and his two children Jeb and Sarah. When he is not being racing cars, he is taking an active role in the environment. Ward established an organization known as the "Ward Burton Wildlife Foundation" in 1996. The Foundation is developing a plan of action to help insure that the nature of native wildlife is preserved for future generations.

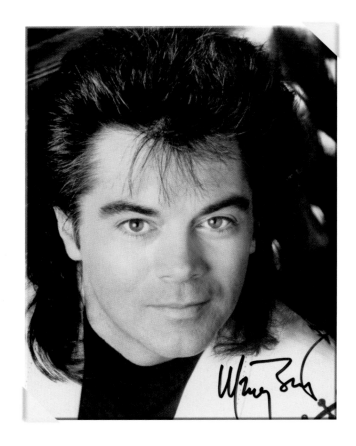

Marty Stuart

Hilda Stuart's Tea Punch

1 qt. boiling water
6 small tea bags

Let boiling water and tea bags stand for 10 minutes.

ADD:
1 1/2 cups sugar
1 small can frozen limeade
1 small can frozen lemonade
Add enough water to make 1 gallon.

Marty was born in Mississippi, but he got his schooling-musical and otherwise-on the road with Lester Flatt and Johnny Cash. He likened his years with Flatt to a high school education and his stint with Cash to earning a university degree. He really did go to high school Flatt, joining the band at 13. His age may have made him some what of a novelty onstage, but his performance on mandolin and guitar was strictly professional quality.

Appetizers & Beverages

Trisha Yearwood

Hot Cheese Dip

1 lb. ground beef, browned & drained
1 brick processed cheese (Velveeta)
1 bottle picante sauce
1 small jar chopped jalapeno peppers

Chop cheese in beef to melt.

Add all other ingredients. Mix well.

Serve warm with tortilla chips.

Vary according to taste by using hot or mild picante sauce and amount of cheese.

Trisha grew up on a farm in Monticello, Georgia, a small town about an hour's drive from Atlanta, Macon, and Athens. Her father, a retired banker, and her mother, a retired schoolteacher, now run Trisha's fan club from there. By the time Trisha was five or six years old she was a big Elvis fan and through high school she absorbed musical influences from all directions, including the country artists of her parents' record collection, southern rock on the radio and school musicals and choral groups.

Paul Overstreet

Lowfat Fruit Drink

7 ripe strawberries
2 peeled bananas
1 hand full of seedless grapes
1 peeled apple
1/2 cup of tofu
1/2 cup of soy milk
1 1/2 cup crushed ice

Blend ingredients in blender.

Paul Overstreet was born in Newton, Mississippi, but grew up in the small town of Vancleave, Mississippi, the youngest of five children born to William and Mary Overstreet.

One night at the movies he saw *Your Cheating Heart* and was amazed that a man could take a guitar and his gift of singing and write down what he was feeling and make a living. He knew right then what he would do with his God given gift. Of course he was side-tracked by sports, but, as he says, he "got over it".

Michael Waltrip

Michael Waltrip's Favorite Meat and Cheese Hors d'oeuvres

1 lb. Ground chuck
1 lb. Sausage - hot or mild
1 lg. pkg. Velveeta cheese
Loaf of cocktail rye bread
   (or any cocktail size
   bread)

Brown beef and sausage, drain, melt Velveeta and mix with meat. Spoon mixture onto bread slices and allow to cool. Store in plastic freezer bags in freezer until ready to serve. To serve, arrange on cookie sheet and broil in oven until cheese bubbles.

Naomi Judd

Orange Tea

2 cups of sugar
2 cups of unsweetened orange
   juice
1/4 cup lemon juice

This is very refreshing. If you use fresh squeezed oranges, scoop out the leftover pulp and serve orange ice in the cleaned out shell.

Boil 15 minutes - 1 quart of water with two cups of sugar. Cool this. Then, add two cups of unsweetened orange juice and 1/4 cup lemon juice. Place in freezer, when mushy remove and beat thoroughly, then refreeze.

Santa's Eggnog

1 dozen eggs (separated)
1/2 lb. powdered sugar
1 qt. Half and Half
1 qt. whipping cream
2 ozs. Napolean brandy
4 ozs. cognac
fresh nutmeg (grate as
    desired)

Ralph Ezell
(Shenandoah)

Add brandy and cognac to egg yolks. Add powdered sugar and beat thoroughly. Refrigerate overnight. Whip whipping cream until thick, then add Half and Half. Add yolk mixture and mix. Whip egg whites and add; mix thoroughly. Grate nutmeg on top and serve.

Stuffed Bacon Rolls

Teddy Gentry
(Alabama)

12 slices bacon
1 medium onion, chopped
2 cloves garlic, minced
1 egg
1/2 cup tomato sauce
3/4 cup soft bread crumbs (1 slice)
1- 4 oz. can sliced mushrooms,
    drained
2 tbsp. snipped parsley
1 lb. ground beef

Partially cook bacon. Drain; reserve 2 tbsp. drippings. Set bacon aside. Cook onion and garlic in reserved drippings till tender but not brown. In bowl combine egg and tomato sauce; stir in bread crumbs, mushrooms, onion mixture, parsley, 1/4 tsp. salt, and 1/8 tsp. pepper. Add meat; mix well. Divide into 4 parts. Place 2 slices bacon side by side on waxed paper. Cut another slice in half crosswise. Place the 2 half-slices at one end of bacon slices, overlapping slightly. Pat 1/4 of meat mixture evenly over bacon; roll up jelly-roll style, starting from narrow end. Place rolls seam side down on rack in 12 x 7 1/2 x 2 inch baking dish. Repeat with remaining bacon and meat. Bake in 350 degree oven for about 40 minutes for medium doneness.

Makes 4 servings.

Cissie Lynn

Taco Dip

1- 8 oz. cream cheese
1- 16 oz. sour cream
1 pkg. Lawrey's Taco Dip
   (or any other brand mix)
chopped lettuce
chopped tomatoes
shredded cheddar cheese
chopped black olives
chopped onions (optional)

MIX:
Mix together the Lawrey's dip, cream cheese, and sour cream.
Spread on a large cookie sheet.

LAYER:
Chopped lettuce, chopped tomatoes, shredded cheddar cheese,
black olives, and onions (optional). Then chill and enjoy!!

Cissie is the daughter of Loretta Lynn, and niece of Crystal Gayle. She spent 1 1/2 years traveling with her mom before going out on her own, and loved every minute of it.

Notes

_____

_____

_____

_____

_____

_____

_____

_____

_____

_____

_____

_____

_____

_____

Breads &
Breakfast

*Breads &
Breakfast*

All Season Bread 19

Banana Nut Bread 20

Banana/Pecan Bread 21

Blaise's Eggs in a Hole 22

Breakfast Casserole 23

Breakfast Tortillas 24

Buttermilk Biscuits 25

Cinnamon Buns 26

Corn Muffins 27

Denver Biscuits 28

"Dutch Baby" 29

Eggs Benedict with Hollandaise Sauce 30

Fried Bread 31

Hag's Hush Puppies 32

Health Muffins 33

Jalapeno Corn Cakes 34

Mexican Cornbread 35

Mexican Cornbread 36

Randy's Mexican Cornbread 37

Tanya's Mexican Cornbread 38

Pumpkin Bread 39

Zucchini Bread 40

Breads & Breakfast

All Season Bread

3 cups All Purpose Flour

2 tsp. soda

1 tsp. salt

1/2 tsp. baking powder

1 1/2 tsp. ground cinnamon

3/4 Cup finely chopped walnuts or
    pecans

3 eggs

2 Cups sugar

3/4 Cup vegetable oil

2 tsp. vanilla

1 8oz. can crushed pineapple

2 Cups prepared fruit or vegetable

Larry & Margaret Fuda

Combine flour, soda, baking powder, cinnamon, and nuts, set aside. Beat eggs lightly in large mixing bowl, add sugar, oil, and vanilla, beat until creamy. Drain crushed pineapple, reserving juice if called for. Stir in pineapple and fruit or vegetable. Add dry ingredients stirring only till moistened. Spoon into 2 well greased and floured 9x5x3" loaf pans. Bake at 350° for 1 hour. Cool in pans 10 minutes, remove to rack to cool.

APPLES: peel and core and shred to make 2 Cups (2 med.)

SWEET POTATOES: peel and shred 2 med. to make 2 cups and use 1 tablespoon reserved pineapple juice.

CARROT: peel and shred to make 2 Cups (2 large) and use 1 tablespoon reserved pineapple juice.

ZUCCHINI: Shred 2 med. to make 2 Cups.

Can be baked in 2 6 Cup Bundt pans for 45 minutes. 2 31lb. shortening cans for 1 hour 15 minutes. 2 7x3 1/2x2" loaf pans 45 to 50 minutes. 8 41/2x21/2x11/2" loaf pans 30 to 35 minutes.

Joe and Mary Bonsall
(The Oak Ridge Boys)

Banana Nut Bread

1/4 cup oil
1 egg, slightly beaten
1 cup sugar
1 1/2 cup sifted flour
1 tsp. soda
1 tsp. salt
1 cup chopped nuts
3 mashed bananas

Combine sugar and oil with egg; stir in dry ingredients;
bake at 350 for 45 to 60 minutes. Makes one large loaf.

Joe's Philadelphia background shows through clearly in his love of pro sports. "I live and die with the Phillies, no matter where they are. 1993 was a great year for me, and one of the highlights was going home to Philadelphia and taking my parents to two World Series games. That was so cool." Joe stays in shape playing tennis, getting on the court nearly every day when he's on the road, with members of the band or crew as opponents. He enjoys the water, both in the Caribbean and closer to home. "

Breads & Breakfast

Banana/Pecan Bread

1 3/4 cup self-rising flour
1/4 cup sugar
1/3 cup margarine
2 egg whites
1 whole egg
2 tbsp. skim milk
2 medium banana, mashed
   (ripe)
1/4 cup chopped pecans

Christy Forester
(Forester Sisters)

Preheat oven to 350 degrees. With mixer, beat sugar and margarine until light and fluffy, scraping sides of bowl often. Add egg, then milk, beating until smooth after each addition. Add flour and bananas alternately to creamed margarine mixture, beating until smooth. Fold in pecans.

Turn batter into an 8 x 4 x 2 inch loaf pan which has been sprayed with vegetable spray. Bake at 350 degrees for 60 minutes or until toothpick comes out clean.

Blaise's Eggs in a Hole

4 slices Italian Bread (1" thick)
4 eggs
hot peppers sliced in oil (Romolo's)
butter

Blaise Alexander

Toast bread lightly. Cut hole in the middle of bread with knife or 4oz. juice glass. Lightly butter both sides of bread and place in frying pan on medium heat. Break egg into hole. Top with 1 tblsp. hot peppers. Cook as desired. Add salt and pepper to taste. You can cover each with a slice of white American cheese if you need to elevate your cholesterol.

Breads & Breakfast

Breakfast Casserole

1 lb. sausage
3 eggs beaten
2 Cups shredded cheese (any kind)
2 packed Cups bread pieces (about 10
    slices)
1 1/2 Cup milk
salt and pepper to taste
(garlic powder and onion optional, to
    taste)

Ryan Newman

Cook and drain sausage.

Mix milk, eggs, salt and pepper together and pour over bread, sausage and cheese in large bowl and mix well. (Mix all together) then: Pour into baking dish and bake at 350° for 1 hour or until brown on top.

Breads & Breakfast

Breakfast Tortillas

1 pkg. of hot beef sausage
6 large eggs
1 small package of Velveeta
   cheese
8 ozs. of sour cream
1 cup of salsa or picante sauce
8 flour tortillas
1 cup chopped onion
salt and pepper to taste

Shelby Lynne

Spray large skillet with no stick cooking spray. Brown sausage until well done. Make room for eggs in skillet. Pour the six large eggs into the skillet and scramble, mixing in with the sausage. Sprinkle chopped velveeta into mixture to melt. Add chopped onion. Pour flour tortillas onto a microwavable plate. Sprinkle the top of the top tortilla with water. Wrap the plate tightly with plastic wrap. Microwave for about 30 seconds. Keep the plate covered until ready to use the tortillas.

When sausage mixture is ready, uncover tortillas. Cover inside of tortillas with sour cream, fill with sausage mixture, top with salsa or picante sauce. Roll up and enjoy!

Breads & Breakfast

Buttermilk Biscuits

2 cups self-rising flour
2 cups buttermilk
one tbsp. lard or cooking oil

Grandpa Jones
(In Memory)

Pour two cups of self-rising flour into a mixing bowl. Pour two cups of buttermilk into a measuring cup. Add one tbsp. of lard or cooking oil to the buttermilk. Pour part of the buttermilk into the flour, kneed it until you have a fairly stiff dough. Mix more buttermilk as needed. When you get the right texture, pour out on a well floured board and roll out to one-half inch thick. Cut out biscuits with a biscuit cutter or glass. Grease a pan well on the bottom and place the biscuits so that they touch each other. That is so they will rise better. Bake in a 400 degree oven about 20 minutes.

If you use plain flour, add 1/4 spoon of soda and 1 tsp. of baking powder to flour.

Cinnamon Buns

2 cups milk
1/2 cup oil
6 tbsp. sugar
1 tbsp. salt
3 pkg. yeast
3/4 cup warm water
2 1/3 quarts plain flour, not self-rising

Bellamy Brothers
(David and Howard)

Combine milk, oil, sugar and salt and heat to lukewarm.
Dissolve yeast in warm water and add. Add flour a little at a
time to form a soft dough. Place in bowl to rise until double in
bulk.

An avid country music fan, Howard and David Bellamy's father would often wake them to the sounds of Merle Haggard or Buck Owens. They grew up surrounded by the harmonies of rhythms of the Jamaican fruit harvesters working in the family's West Central Florida's orange groves during the day. Exposure to Elvis, Ricky Nelson, Buddy Holly and the Everly Brothers as well as the British invasion and the Cultural Revolution in the 60's resulted in their highly individualistic style and sound they have taken on the road for more than 20 years.

Corn Muffins

1 cup whole wheat flour
1 cup yellow corn meal
4 tsp. baking powder
1/2 tsp. salt (optional)
1/4 cup sugar
2 eggs lightly beaten
1 cup skim milk
3 tbsp. butter, melted
1 cup cream style corn

Linda Ronstadt

In a large bowl, combine the first 5 ingredients.

In a medium bowl, combine the eggs, milk, butter and corn. Add this to the dry ingredients, stirring until the dry ingredients are moistened.

Spoon the batter into 12 greased muffin cups. Bake in a preheated oven at 425 degrees for 20-25 minutes or until the tops are golden.

Leroy Van Dyke

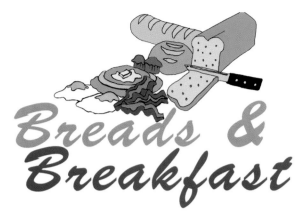

Denver Biscuits

from the kitchen of Irene Sims Van Dyke, mother of Leroy Van Dyke

1 pkg. yeast
1/4 cup warm water
(soften active dry yeast in water)

4 cups milk, scalded
1 cup shortening (lard)
1/2 cup sugar
After you scald the milk, add the lard
    and sugar, then let it cool.
Add to the above:
dissolved yeast mixture
1 cup mashed potatoes
2 tsp. salt
1 level tsp. baking soda
2 heaping tsp. baking powder

Then add enough sifted all-purpose flour to make a soft dough. (For whole wheat biscuits or rolls, I use half all-purpose flour and half whole wheat flour).

Place in large, lightly greased bowl, cover and store in refrigerator; use dough as needed. Punch down if rises too much. Dough will keep for several days in the refrigerator. When you are ready to make the biscuits, pull off the amount of dough you need, put on lightly floured surface, knead gently for a few seconds. Roll dough to 1/2 inch thick; cut with biscuit cutter. Place on greased cookie sheet, cover and let stand 10 minutes or longer. Bake in hot oven (400 degrees) 10 to 12 minutes. This dough also makes excellent cinnamon rolls!

"Dutch Baby"

4 eggs
1 cup milk
1 cup flour
1/2 stick of butter

Doug and Ricky Lee Phelps
(Brother Phelps)

Preheat oven to 450 degrees.

Melt butter in cast iron skillet. Mix all ingredients together in a bowl.
Pour into skillet. Bake at 450 degrees for 20 minutes.

Top with butter and powdered sugar or honey, jam, etc.

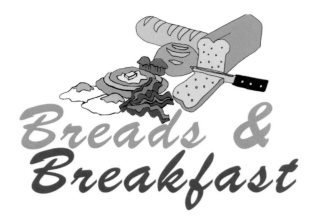

Eggs Benedict with Hollandaise Sauce

Eggs
Fresh lemon
Butter
English Muffins
Canadian Bacon

Ward Burton

Hollandaise Sauce:

Combine 2 tablespoons of fresh squeezed lemon juice and 2 egg yolks in a small bowl and beat with a fork. Put a stick of butter in a small saucepan over low heat. Pour the egg/lemon mixture in the saucepan and stir continuously until all the butter is melted. Allow to thicken and immediately remove from heat.

Cut the English muffins in half and butter. Place one slice of Canadian bacon on each muffin and warm in oven just enough to melt butter. Poach eggs and place on top of muffins. Pour Hollandaise sauce over muffins and serve.

Breads & Breakfast

Fried Bread

4 cups flour
1 1/4 tsp. salt
3 tsp. baking powder
salad oil for frying
3 tbsp. sugar
2 tbsp. shortening
1 1/4 cup milk

Tracy Lynne

Sift flour, measure and sift again with salt, baking powder and sugar. Cut in the shortening and add milk to make a soft dough just firm enough to roll. Cover bowl and let dough stand for 30-60 minutes. Then roll 1/4 inch thick on lightly floured board and cut into small shapes. Fry in 1 (one) inch of oil.

Should make 4 dozen.

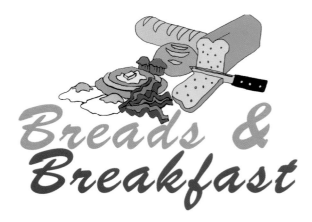

Breads & Breakfast

Hag's Hush Puppies

2 cups cornmeal
1 tbsp. flour
1/2 tsp. baking soda
1 tsp. salt
1 egg, beaten
3 tbsp. chopped onion
1 cup buttermilk

Merle Haggard

Mix all dry ingredients. Add egg, onion and buttermilk. Mix well and drop by spoonfuls into deep, hot fat. (360 degrees.) When they float, they are done. Drain on paper toweling and serve hot. Makes about 25 hush puppies.

Maverick country singer Merle Haggard represents an unusual intersection in American music, a crossroad where folk, pop, jazz and blues traditions are used to create his own soul-baring form of expression.

Breads & Breakfast

Health Muffins

2 1/2 cups oat bran
1/2 cup brown sugar
2 tsp. cinnamon
1 tbsp. baking powder
1/2 cup chopped walnuts
1/2 cup raisins
1/2 cup skim milk or evaporated
    skim milk
3/4 cup frozen apple-juice
    concentrate
2 eggs whites
2 tbsp. vegetable oil
1 medium cored and chopped apple
2/3 medium orange
(wash peeling thoroughly and slice and chop rind and a little of the
    orange with the rind)

Donna Fargo

Mix the dry ingredients in a large bowl. Mix the milk, apple-juice concentrate, egg whites, and oil in a bowl or blender. Add to the dry ingredients and mix. Add chopped apple. Line the muffin pans with paper baking cups and fill with batter. Bake in a 425 degree oven for 17 to 20 minutes. Makes 12 or 13 muffins.

After cooling, store in a large plastic bag to retain moisture and softness.

Good with your favorite jelly, applesauce or apple butter or honey or just plain.

Christy Forester
(Forester Sisters)

Jalapeno Corn Cakes

1 1/2 cup self-rising cornmeal
1 cup creamed corn
1/2 cup buttermilk
1/2 cup vegetable oil
1 cup Monterey Jack cheese,
　shredded
2 tsp. jalapeno pepper, finely
　chopped
1 egg
3 green onions, (green part only),
　finely chopped
butter

In mixing bowl blend together the cornmeal, corn, buttermilk, vegetable oil, cheese, jalapeno pepper, egg and green onions. Heat griddle or skillet, butter it and place 2 oz. ladlefuls onto the griddle or skillet. Cook until bubbles come to the surface and flip them over onto the other side and cook for a few minutes more.

Breads & Breakfast

Mexican Cornbread

1 cup corn meal (self rising)
1/2 cup flour
1/2 tsp. sugar
milk - enough to make
    mixture moist
1 can cream style corn
1/2 cup jalapeno pepper
1 lb. hamburger

Johnny Rodriguez

Mix cornbread as directed, set aside. Brown hamburger meat, set aside. To cornbread mixture, add corn and peppers. Place 1/2 mixture in bottom of casserole dish, then add hamburger. Put rest of mix on top and sprinkle with cheese. Bake at 400 degrees for 30 to 45 minutes.

Hank Thompson

Mexican Cornbread

Wet Ingredients:

2/3 Cup Buttermilk
1/2 Cup oil
1 8oz. can cream style corn
1 4ox. jar chopped pimentos
1 Cup grated cheddar cheese
2 eggs
1 or 2 chopped jalapeno peppers

Blend all together. You may double or quadruple the above and freeze it in convenient portions. Then thaw and add dry ingredients below:

Dry Ingredients:

1 Cup yellow corn meal
1 tsp. salt
1 tsp. soda

Preheat skillet on burn with a little oil. When hot, pour in combined mixture and slightly brown on bottom. Put in preheated oven of 350° for 30-40 minutes. Then switch to brioler and brown on top. YUM!YUM!

Breads & Breakfast

Randy's Mexican Cornbread

1 pkg. Martha White Mexican
    Corn Bread Mix
2 cups self rising meal
3 eggs, beaten
1/3 cup oil
1 1/2 cup milk
1- 16 oz. can cream style corn
1/2 cup chopped spring onions and
    tops
1/4 cup chopped green pepper
1 tbsp. jalapeno pepper, mashed
2 cups cooked sausage, crumbled
1/2 tsp. red pepper, crushed
2 tbsp. pimento

Randy Travis

Mix all ingredients. Preheat heavy iron skillet with about 6 tbsp. oil (or bacon drippings) until very hot. Pour mixture into pan. Bake at 375 degrees for 20 to 30 minutes or until done.

Leftover sausage may be used as garnish on top.

Tanya's Mexican Cornbread

Tanya Tucker

1 1/2 cup self-rising cornmeal
1 can golden corn
3 eggs
1 cup grated cheese
1 hot pepper, chopped
1 cup buttermilk
1/2 cup oil
3/4 cup chopped green pepper

Mix half oil and other ingredients. Pour remaining oil in skillet. Pour cornbread mixture into hot skillet. Bake at 375 degrees until brown.

Tanya Tucker has been entertaining audiences since she was a child. She had a demo record by the age of 9. Her hit "Delta Dawn" at age 13 was one of the biggest hits in country music history. Tanya had a Grammy nomination, a Greatest Hits package, and was on the cover of Rolling Stone Magazine by the time she was 15.

Pumpkin Bread

2/3 cup shortening
2 2/3 cups sugar
4 eggs
1 can (pound) pumpkin
2/3 cup water
3 1/3 cups flour*
2 tsp. soda
1 1/2 tsp salt
1/2 tsp. baking powder
1 tsp. cinnamon
1 tsp. cloves
2/3 cup coarsely chopped nuts

Crystal Gayle

Heat oven to 350 degrees. Grease two 9 x 5 x 3-inch loaf pans or three 8 1/2 x 4 1/2 x 2 1/2 inch loaf pans. In large bowl, cream shortening and sugar until fluffy. Stir in eggs, pumpkin and water. Blend in flour, soda, salt, baking powder, cinnamon and cloves. Stir in nuts.

Pour into pans. Bake 70 minutes or until toothpick inserted in center comes out clean.

* If using self-rising flour, omit soda, salt and baking powder.

Donnie Allison

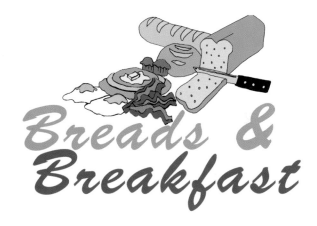

Zucchini Bread

1 cup oil
3 eggs
1 2/3 cups white sugar
1/3 cup brown sugar
3 tsp. vanilla
2 cups zucchini, raw grated
3 cups flour
1 tsp. salt
1 tsp. soda
1/2 tsp. baking powder
3 tsp. cinnamon
1/2 cup chopped pecans

Beat together oil, eggs, sugars, and vanilla for 2 minutes with electric mixer. Stir in grated zucchini. In separate bowl, sift flour, salt, soda, bakin powder, and cinnamon. Mix together for about 1 minute then stir in chopped nuts.

Bake in 2 greased & floured loaf pans. Cook in oven for 1 hour at 350 degrees. Enjoy!

Donnie's three sons, Kenny, Ronald and Donald are Legacy racecar builders. His daughter Pam is married to race driver Hut Stricklin. Donnie enjoys playing golf, hunting, fishing and being with his family.

Cakes

Cakes

Angel Food Cake 43

Baby Food Cake 44

Best Yet Cake 45

Cheese Cake 46

Chocolate Cake 47

Chocolate Pound Cake With Chocolate Icing 48

Coconut Cake 49

Coconut Cake 50

Coconut Pound Cake 51

Dump Cake 52

Friendship Cake 53

Layered Chocolate Dessert Cake 54

Mountain Pound Cake 56

Old Fashioned Tea Cakes 57

Punch Bowl Cake 58

Red Velvet Cake 59

The Farmer's Daughter's Carrot Cake 60

Torta Dipere (Tuscan Pear Cake) 61

Tropical Fruit Delight Cake 62

Cakes

Angel Food Cake

1 1/2 cup egg whites
1tsp. cream of tarter
1 1/2 cups of sugar
1/4 tsp. salt
1 cup flour (sifted) then sift
    4 times
1 tsp. vanilla

Richard Petty

Beat egg whites until foamy, add cream of tartar and beat until stiff, but not dry. Gradually beat in sugar. Add vanilla, then fold in flour as gently as possible. Bake in angel food pan at 325 degrees for 1 hour and 15 minutes or until top is nicely browned.

Cakes

John Andretti

Baby Food Cake

Mix together:
3 eggs
1 1/2 cup salad oil
2 tsp. cinnamon
1 1/2 tsp. baking soda
1 tsp. salt
1 1/4 tsp. vanilla
2 cups sugar

Add strained baby food:
1 4 1/2 oz. jar carrots
1 4 1/2 oz. jar apricots with tapioca
1 4 oz. applesauce
2 cups flour

Mix and bake on jelly roll pan (15x10) 350° for 30 to 40 minutes. Frost when cool with:
1 8oz. pkg. cream cheese
1 stick oleo
1 1-lb. box confectioners sugar
2 tsp. vanilla

Add nuts to frosting or sprinkle on top.

Cakes

Best Yet Cake

2 cups all-purpose flour
2 cups sugar
2 eggs
2 tsp. baking soda
1- 20 oz. can crushed
   pineapple
   (undrained)

Ricky & Sharon White Skaggs

Mix all ingredients by hand. Pour into a greased and floured
13x9x2 inch pan. Bake at 350 degrees for 35 minutes.

FROSTING:
1- 8 oz. pkg. cream cheese softened
1- 1/2 cup confectioners sugar
1/2 stick margarine
1 tsp. vanilla
1 cup chopped pecans (reserved for top)

Cheese Cake

1 - 8oz. pkg. cream cheese
1/2 cup sugar
2 cups cool whip

Mark Smith

Whip cream cheese & sugar. Add cool whip and pour into
unbaked graham cracker crust (9"). Top with one can
Cherry Pie filling.

Cakes

Chocolate Cake

1 cup butter or margarine
2 cups sugar
2 eggs
1 tsp. vanilla
3 cups sifted flour
1/2 cup cocoa
2 tsp. soda
1 tsp. salt
2 cups buttermilk

Charlie Daniels

Grease and flour two 9-inch layer cake pans or one large sheet cake pan. Cream butter, gradually beat in sugar until fluffy. Add eggs one at a time. Beat well about 2 minutes. Add vanilla. Add sifted dry ingredients alternately with buttermilk using low speed of mixer. Pour into pans. Bake at 350 degrees for 35-40 minutes. Remove from pans after a few minutes. Cool on rack. Frost with Chocolate Butter Frosting.

CHOCOLATE BUTTER FROSTING

1 box confectioners sugar
1/2 cup cocoa
1/8 tsp. salt
1/4 lb. butter or margarine (room temperature)
1 tsp. vanilla
5-7 tbsp. milk

Mix all ingredients together and beat on low speed until smooth. Spread on cool cake. This icing tastes better after it sits on cake for about one hour.

Alan Jackson

Chocolate Pound Cake With Chocolate Icing

3 cups sifted plain flour
1/2 cup cocoa
1- 1/4 cup sweet milk
6 eggs
1/2 tsp. baking powder
3 cup sugar
1/2 cup Crisco
2 sticks margarine
2 tsp. vanilla
1/4 tsp. salt

Mix sugar, Crisco and margarine. Add eggs one at a time. Mix well. Gradually add dry ingredients alternately with milk. Add vanilla. Pour mixture into large greased and floured tube pan. Bake at 325 degrees for 1 1/2 hours.

CHOCOLATE ICING
1/2 cup butter flavored Crisco
2 cups sugar
1/4 cup cocoa
2/3 cup sweet milk
1/4 tsp. salt
1 tsp. vanilla

Put all ingredients in a boiler. Bring to a boil, stirring constantly. Boil 3 minutes. Will thicken quickly as it cools. Ice cake while icing is still warm. If it gets too thick before you can get it on cake, add small amount of hot water.

Cakes

Coconut Cake

1 box white or yellow cake
  mix
1- 15 oz. can Cream of
  Coconut
1- 14 oz. can Eagle Brand
  Milk
1 small bowl LaCreme
1 small bag coconut

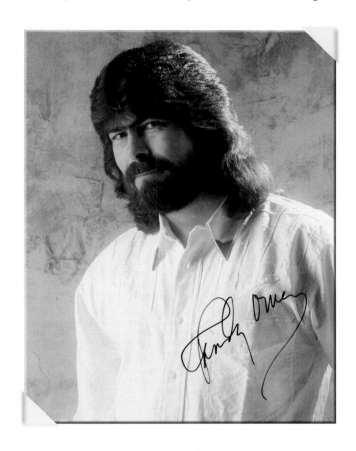

Randy Owen
(Alabama)

Mix cake according to directions on package and bake in 9x13 pan. Let cool, then puncture top full of holes. Fill holes with mixture of Cream of Coconut and Eagle Brand. Top with LaCreme and then the coconut. Must keep refrigerated. Absolutely delicious!

Coconut Cake

1 box white cake mix
2 cups sour cream
2 cups coconut
1/2 tsp. almond flavoring

Naomi Judd

This coconut cake is so moist, and not too sweet with the use of sour cream.

Use one box of white cake mix. Follow directions on box making two layers. When layers are baked and cooled, split each layer, making four layers.

Mix together the following for filling and icing:

2 cups sour cream
2 cups sugar
2 cups coconut
1/2 tsp. almond flavoring

After mixing thoroughly, spread between layers, on top and sides.

Refrigerate overnight. Must be kept refrigerated.

Cakes

Larry Stewart

Coconut Pound Cake

5 eggs, beaten
2 cups sugar
1 cup Wesson Oil
2 cups flour
1 1/2 tsp. baking powder
1/2 tsp. salt
1/2 cup milk
1 tsp. vanilla
1 tsp. coconut extract
1 can angel flake coconut

Blend eggs and sugar. Add oil. Add flour, baking powder and salt. Add milk, vanilla, coconut extract and coconut. Put in greased and floured tube cake pan. Bake at 350 degrees for 1 hour or longer.

SAUCE:
1 cup sugar
1/2 cup water
1/4 cup oleo
1 tsp. coconut extract

Boil 1 minute and pour over warm cake. Let cool and remove from pan.

Cakes

Jimmy O
(Diamond Rio)

Dump Cake

1 box yellow cake mix
1- 12 oz. crushed
    pineapple
1- 21 oz. cherry pie filling
1 stick butter
1 cup chopped nuts

Preheat oven to 350 degrees. In a normal sized baking pan dump the undrained pineapple into a greased pan. Dump on top of the pineapple the cherry pie filling and on top of that the yellow cake mix. Spread the nuts on top with eight slices of butter placed on top of the nuts.

DO NOT MIX OR STIR ANYTHING AT ANYTIME!!

Baked uncovered for fifty minutes, let cool and serve.

This is one of Jimmy O's favorite recipes to make.

Cakes

Friendship Cake

First Day:
2 1/2 Cups sugar
1 (No. 303) can sliced peaches with juice
Tenth Day:
2 1/2 Cups sugar
1 (No. 303) can pineapple chunks and
    juice
Twentieth Day:
 2 1/2 Cups sugar
2 (9oz.) jars maraschino cherries (without
    juice)
Cake: 1 box yellow cake mix (without
    pudding mix)
2/3 Cup Crisco oil
1 1/2 Cup drained fruit
1 box instant vanilla pudding
4 eggs
1 Cup chopped pecans

Barbara Fairchild

First Day: In a gallon jug, mix 1 1/2 cups starter juice from peaches. Cut peaches into smaller pieces; add sugar. Add to starter juice. Do not put in icebox. Stir daily.

On day 10, cut pineapple into smaller pieces; add pineapple and sugar to jug. Stir daily.

On day 20, cut cherries in halves. Add cherries and sugar to jug stir daily.

On day 13, you are ready to make cakes. You will have enough fruit for 3 Bundt cakes or 6 small loaf cakes or 9 smaller aluminum pans from grocery store.

Cake: Mix cake mix, pudding, oil, and eggs together. It will be thick until thoroughly mixed. Fold in drained fruit and chopped nuts. Grease pans; pour in mixture. Bake at 350° for 40 minutes or 60 minutes depending on pan size. All cakes need not be made the same day, but stir daily the leftover mixture until all are made, or freeze. Let the cake stand 10 minutes after removing from oven.

You will have juice to give to 3 friends. Be sure to save 1 1/2 cups for yourself. Do not keep lid on jar too tight. This entire recipe takes 3 boxes of cake mix, 3 boxes instant pudding and three cups chopped nuts.

Cakes

Doug Supernaw

Layered Chocolate Dessert Cake

1 1/2 cups milk
4 squares unsweetened chocolate
1 1/2 cups sugar
1/2 cup butter
1 tsp. vanilla extract
2 eggs
2 cups sifted all-purpose flour
3/4 teaspoon salt
1 tsp. baking soda
1 recipe Mocha Butter Cream
1/2 recipe Special Chocolate Icing

Line bottom of 13 x 8 x 2-inch baking pan with waxed paper; grease and flour the waxed paper.

Place 1 cup milk, chocolate, and 1/2 cup sugar in top of double boiler. Place over boiling water; cook, stirring constantly, until chocolate is melted. Remove from boiling water; cool.

Cream the butter and remaining sugar in large mixing bowl with electric mixer. Add vanilla and eggs; beat well. Beat in chocolate mixture.

Sift flour with salt; add to chocolate mixture alternately with remaining milk. Beat 2 minutes at medium speed.

Dissolve soda in 3 tablespoons boiling water. Add to batter; beat 1 minute. Pour into prepared pan.

Bake at 350 degrees 30 to 35 minutes or until cake tests done. Cool in pan 10 minutes. Remove from pan; cool on rack.

(continued on page 55)

Cakes

(LAYERED CHOCOLATE DESSERT CAKE, continued)

Trim edges from cake; cut cake crosswise into 3 equal portions. Cover 2 portions with Mocha Butter Cream , top third portion with Special Chocolate Icing.

MOCHA BUTTER CREAM
1 cup butter, softened
6 cups sifted confectioners' sugar
3 egg yolks
1/4 cup Basic Coffee Syrup
2 squares semi-sweet chocolate, melted

Cream butter in large mixing bowl with electric mixer until light and fluffy. Add half the sugar; beat until smooth. Add egg yolks; blend well. Mix in remaining confectioners' sugar. Add Coffee Syrup and chocolate; beat until well combined and fluffy. Yield enough to fill, frost and decorate 9-inch cake.

SPECIAL CHOCOLATE ICING
1/2 cup light corn syrup
6 tablespoons water
5 tablespoons butter
1 (12-ounce) package semi-sweet chocolate bits

Combine corn syrup, water, and butter in saucepan. Bring to rapid boil, stirring until butter is melted. Remove from heat; add chocolate. Stir until chocolate is completely melted. Cool to room temperature before pouring over cake, petis fours, or desired dessert to glaze; chill until set.

Yield about 2 1/2 cups.

Cakes

The Statler Brothers
*(Johnny Fortune, Harold Reid,
Don Reid, Phil Balsley)*

Mountain Pound Cake

1/2 lb. butter (2 sticks)
1/2 cup Crisco (Crisco
   only)
3 cups sugar
5 eggs
3 cups plain flour
1/2 tsp. baking powder
1 cup milk
1 1/2 tsp. vanilla
1/2 tsp. lemon (if desired)

Cream butter, shortening and sugar. Add eggs one at a time. Add flour and milk alternately; add baking powder with the last of flour. Add flavoring. Pour into 10 inch tube pan (greased and floured). Place in "Cold Oven". Turn over to 350 degrees F. Bake 1 hour and 15 minutes. DO NOT OPEN OVEN EVEN ONCE. Let stand a few minutes before removing from pan.

Cakes

Old Fashioned Tea Cakes

9 cups self-rising
    flour
6 eggs
3 cups sugar
2 1/2 cups
    shortening
2 1/2 tsp. vanilla
1/2 cup sweet milk

Charlie Daniels

Mix well in a large bowl - like making biscuits. Roll out and
cut with a round biscuit cutter.
Bake at 300° until light brown.

This recipe came from Mrs. Idabell McMillan, who is the mother of one of my
childhood schoolmates. It's one of my favorites!

Cakes

Ronnie McDowell

Punch Bowl Cake

1 pkg. yellow cake mix
   (Jiffy)
1 small pkg. vanilla instant
   pudding
1 large can crushed
   pineapple, drained
1 can cherry pie filling
1 container cool whip
pecans

Bake cake as directed on package. Break into small pieces in bottom of bowl.

Mix putting as directed and pour over cake. Put pineapple on the pudding. Next put cherry pie filling and then cool whip, add nuts on top if desired. This makes a great dessert for Christmas.

Cakes

Red Velvet Cake

Joe Diffie

2 eggs
1 1/2 cups Wesson oil
1 1/2 cups sugar with 1 tsp. cocoa
2 1/2 cups flour with 1/2 tsp. salt
1 cup buttermilk with tsp. soda
1 tsp. vinegar
1 tsp. vanilla
2 oz. red food coloring

Mix together and bake at 350 degrees for 30 minutes or until tested done. Cool.

FOR ICING:
1 box powdered sugar
1/2 stick oleo
8 oz. pkg. cream cheese (set out to soften)
1 tsp. vanilla
1 1/2 cups chopped pecans

Merle Haggard

The Farmer's Daughter's Carrot Cake

2 cups sugar
1 1/2 cups Crisco Oil
4 eggs
2 cups finely grated carrots
1- 8 oz. can crushed pineapple
1/2 cup chopped walnuts
2 cups flour
2 tsp. baking powder
2 tsp. soda
1 tsp. salt
2 tsp. cinnamon

Beat sugar, oil and eggs together. Add carrots, pineapple, and nuts. Sift together dry ingredients and blend into mixture. Bake in a 350 degree oven. For a sheet cake, bake 40 minutes. For a 2 layer cake, bake approximately 30 minutes. Test with toothpick.

Cakes

Torta Dipere
(Tuscan Pear Cake)

2 tbls. butter
1/3 cup fine amaretti crumbs
1 lb. ripe Bosc pears
1/3 cup dark rum
4 eggs
1 1/2 cups granulated sugar
3 cups flour
2 tsp. baking powder
1/2 tsp. salt
1/4 cup confectioners' sugar

Troy Beebe

Preheat oven to 350°F. Grease an 8-inch springform pan with butter; dust all over with amaretti crumbs.

Quarter unpeeled pears; core them and cut them into slices 1/8 inch thick. Put slices in a ceramic, glass, or stainless steel bowl and add rum. Toss gently to blend and set aside for a few minutes.

Beat eggs and granulated sugar in an electric mixer on high speed until light and fluffy. Sift together flour, baking powder, and salt. Fold flour mixture into egg mixture by hand. Place half the pear slices on the bottom of the prepared pan; cover with batter and arrange the remaining pear slices on top. Bake 20 minutes; quickly dust top with confectioners' sugar and return to oven until cake is well browned and a tester inesrted in the center comes out clean, about another 20 minutes.

Serve warm. Serves 4 to 6.

Cakes

Tropical Fruit Delight Cake

1 box butter cake mix
1 can 11oz. mandarin
   oranges and juice
1/2 cup oil
4 eggs

Barbara Mandrell

Mix all ingredients together in bowl. Bake at 325° about 30 to 35 minutes.

Frosting:
1 pkg (3oz.) vanilla instant pudding mix (use dry)
1 cup (9oz. carton) Cool Whip
1 can (large) crushed pineapple with juice

Mix together in bowl. Spread on cooled cake. Refrigerate.

(If a regular cake mix is used, add about 1/2 cup melted margarine to other ingredients in the cake mix.)

After cake is cooled, stick holes in it with a fork to enable frosting to "soak" in the cake.

Casseroles

Casseroles

All In One Casserole 65

Bacon-Cheese-Tomato Pie 66

Baked Macaroni & Beef 67

Broccoli and Cheese Quiche 68

Chicken and Rice Casserole 69

Chicken & Rice Casserole 70

Chicken Spaghetti 71

Chicken & Broccoli Casserole 72

Chicken Broccoli and Wild Rice Casserole 73

Chicken Salad Casserole 74

Chille Relleno Casserole 75

Egg Plant Rollatini 76

Green Bean Casserole 77

Green Chile Quiche 78

Green Rice 79

Hal Ketchem's Favorite Casserole 80

Meatball and Cabbage Casserole 81

Megan's Broccoli Rice Casserole 82

Mexican Coo 83

Mom's Chicken Casserole 84

Pineapple Casserole 85

Pork Chop Casserole 86

Raymone's Beanie Weenies 87

Risto Alla Milanese (Lemon Risotto) 88

Spanish Rice And Chicken Casserole 89

Squash Casserole 90

Vegetable Casserole 91

Casseroles

All In One Casserole

Ted Musgrave

1 1/2 lbs. ground beef
1 - 15oz. can vegetables (your choice)
   drained
1 - can Cream of Celery *or* Mushroom
   Soup
1 - 8oz. bag shredded cheddar cheese
1 - box Hungry Jack Mashed Potatoes
2 eggs

- Preheat oven to 350 degrees
- Brown ground beef in skillet, drain
- In large bowl, mix beef with soup and vegetables
- Spread evenly in 9x13 pan
- Prepare 6 servings of potatoes according to directions on box, add two eggs,
mix well.
- Spread potatoes evenly over beef mixture
- Sprinkle with cheese and bake until cheese melts and bubbles, approximately
20-25 minutes.

Casseroles

Louise Mandrell

Bacon-Cheese-Tomato Pie

Pastry for 8" - 9", 2 crust pie
  (Pillsbury All-Ready Pie
  Crusts)
8 oz. bacon, fried
2/3 cup each onion & green bell
  peppers, chopped
4 tomatoes, sliced (peeled if you
  like)
6 oz. shredded cheddar cheese
6 oz. shredded mozzarella cheese
Tabasco
1 tbsp. milk

Line pie plate with half of pastry (one circle) and prick bottom. Break bacon into large pieces and place half of pieces on bottom of pie shell; cover with 1/3 cup each of onion and bell pepper. Cover with 1/2 of tomato slices; sprinkle with tabasco. Next, cover with cheddar cheese. Repeat these layers starting with remaining bacon and finishing with mozzarella cheese. Place remaining pastry circle on top, dampening edge of pastry and pressing edges together. Make several slits on top, and decorate with pastry leaves made from trimmings if you like. Glaze with the milk, and bake for 35 minutes. When serving, if there is a lot of juice on the bottom of the pie, just drain after you've cut and removed your first slice. This dish is excellent in the summer when made with homegrown tomatoes and bell peppers.

Casseroles

Baked Macaroni & Beef

1 small box macaroni
2 cans of diced tomatoes
2 lbs. ground beef
1 tsp. oregano
2 cloves of garlic minced
Salt & pepper to taste
Shredded cheese (use cheddar & jack)

Hut Stricklin

Fry ground beef and separate finely. Cook macaroni according to box and drain. Add macaroni to ground beef. Add all other ingredients and heat completely. Pour into a baking dish and cover with shredded cheese. Bake at 350 degrees until cheese bubbles.

**Serve with garlic bread or salad.

Casseroles

Ward Burton

**Broccoli and Cheese
Quiche**

Pie crust
1/2 cup fresh chopped broccoli
1/2 cup grated cheddar cheese
1/2 cup grated parmesan cheese
4 eggs
1/4 cup milk
2 tbsp. butter
dash of salt and pepper

Preheat oven to 350 and bake pie crust until golden. Remove pie crust from oven. Steam broccoli until desired tenderness. Mix remaining ingredients well and pour into pie crust. Bake at 350 for 20 minutes or until done. Do not over bake.

Chicken and Rice Casserole

4-6 skinned chicken breasts
1 can of cream of chicken soup
1 1/2 cup of dry rice
salt & pepper

Duane & Norah Lee Allen
(The Oak Ridge Boys)

In a medium casserole dish, add dry rice, soup and 1 1/2 cans of water and stir; make mixture soupy.

Rinse and drain chicken pieces and lay on top of rice mixture.

Add salt and pepper. Cover with aluminum foil and bake at 325 degrees for approximately 1 hour. Serve with a salad or vegetable and your favorite bread.

Ronnie McDowell

Chicken & Rice Casserole

1 1/2 cups rice
1 can cream of chicken soup
1 can cream of celery soup
1 stick margarine
1 1/2 cup milk
1 chicken cooked & deboned
1/4 cup onion, chopped
Salt and pepper to taste

Place rice in casserole dish, mix milk and soups together. Add half of this to rice, stir. Add 1/2 of butter and onions. Add chicken. Then add rest of soup, butter and onions. Sprinkle top with cracker crumbs. Bake 45 minutes at 350 degrees.

Casseroles

Ken & Ann Schrader

Chicken Spaghetti

10 to 12 chicken breasts
1 lb. vermicelli spaghetti
2 lb. box Velveeta cheese
1 can Rotel tomatoes and
    green chilies
2 tbsp. worcestershire sauce
1 jar drained mushrooms
1 can LaSuer peas
2 lg. green peppers,
    chopped
2 lg. onions, chopped
1/4 cup butter

Place chicken in large pot and cover with 3 quarts water. Salt and pepper to taste. Bring to a boil and cook until tender. Cool chicken. Save broth. Cut chicken into chunks.

Cook vermicelli in broth. When done, add cheese (cut into chunks) to broth and vermicelli. Stir until melted. Add tomatoes, worcestershire sauce, mushrooms, peas and chicken.

Saute peppers and onions in butter. Add to pot. Pour contents into one large casserole or smaller casseroles to freeze. To serve, bake at 350 degrees for 45 minutes (or longer if frozen).
Yield: 16 servings.

Casseroles

Ray Herndon
(McBride & The Ride)

Chicken & Broccoli Casserole

1 pkg. frozen broccoli
2 tbsp. sherry
3/4 cup sharp cheddar
　　cheese, shredded
2 tsp. lemon juice
3 cups of condensed cream
　　of chicken soup
1 1/2 cups mayonnaise
3/4 cup soft bread crumbs
2 tbsp. melted butter

Arrange cooked broccoli in a 9" x 13" pan. Cut chicken into bite size pieces and place over broccoli. Mix together soup, mayonnaise, lemon juice and sherry and pour over broccoli and chicken. Sprinkle with cheese and bread crumbs and drizzle melted butter over top. Bake covered at 350 degrees for one hour - until bubbly and very hot.

Casseroles

Chicken Broccoli and Wild Rice Casserole

1- 6 oz. pkg. long grain rice
1- 10 oz. pkg. frozen chopped
    broccoli
2 cups cubed chicken, ham, or
    turkey, cooked
1- 4 oz. can sliced mushrooms,
    drained
1 can water chestnuts, drained & sliced
1 cup shredded extra sharp cheddar
    cheese
1 can cream of celery soup
1 cup mayonnaise
2 tsp. prepared mustard
1 tsp. curry powder
1/2 cup Parmesan cheese

Alice Detrick

Cook broccoli and rice. Spread rice in 9 x 13-1/2" pan, broccoli on top, with meat, mushrooms, water chestnuts and cheddar cheese over the broccoli. Blend the soup, mayonnaise, mustard, curry together and spoon over the other ingredients. Sprinkle Parmesan cheese on top. Bake at 350 degrees for 45 minutes.

Serves 8.

Casseroles

Chicken Salad Casserole

Emmylou Harris

1 chicken (about 3 1/2 lbs.)
6 cups water
1 tsp. salt
6 peppercorns
1- 10 3/4 oz. can condensed cream of
    mushroom soup
1/4 cup mayonnaise
1 cup diced celery
1/4 cup minced onion
3/4 cup potato chips (crushed)
1/2 cup grated sharp cheese

Place chicken in a large saucepan with enough water to just cover it. Add salt and peppercorns. Bring to a boil. Lower heat, cover and simmer until the chicken is tender, about 45 minutes. Remove chicken from the liquid. Remove skin and bones and dice the meat.

Mix chicken with all the ingredients except the potato chips and grated cheese. Put into a greased (lightly) 1 1/2 quart round or square casserole dish. Bake casserole at 325 degrees for 40 minutes. Sprinkle with crushed potato chips and grated sharp cheese and bake 10 minutes longer.

Yield about 4-6 servings.

Casseroles

Chille Relleno
Casserole

2 cans green chilli peppers (7oz. cans)
   or 4 (4oz. cans)
1 lb. graded cheddar cheese
1 lb. grated monterey jack cheese
1 - 13oz. can evaporated milk
3 tbsp. flour
4 eggs
1 tsp. salt
2 cans (8oz.) tomato sauce or tomato salsa

Johnny Rutherford

Wash and remove seeds from chillis and drain (pat dry with paper towels).
Separate eggs.
Beat egg yolks, milk, flour, and salt together.
Beat egg whites in separate bowl until nice and frothy.
Fold mixtures together.

Line bottom of casserole (2 1/2 qt.) with chillis.
Add layer of cheeses, layer of chillis, layer of cheese.
Pour milk and egg mixture over this mixture.

Bake at 325 degrees for 1 hour. Pour salsa over top and bake 30 minutes longer, Let cool at least 30 minutes before serving.

(Note: You can also add a mixture of lean ground beef (drained) and sliced mushrooms
 between layers or sliced (shredded) chicken breasts (cooked).)

75

Kathy Mattea

Casseroles

Egg Plant Rollatini

1- 2 lb. eggplant
6 oz. chilled mozzarella
tomato sauce
1 3/4 oz. romano, cut in 1" pieces
4 eggs
1/4 cup water
3/4 tsp. salt
3/4 cup all-purpose flour
vegetable oil (for frying)
1 cup fresh spinach leaves
1 15 oz. carton ricotta cheese, drained

Peel eggplant. Cut eggplant lengthwise into at least 12- 1/8 inch thick slices, discarding rounded pieces. (Shredder) Shred mozzarella using light pressure. Remove from work bowl. (Steel knife) Process romano until minced. Remove 1/2 of cheese from work bowl and set aside. Add 3 eggs, water and 1/4 tsp. salt to work bowl and mix till combined, 5 seconds. Transfer egg mixture to pie plate. Place flour in second pie plate. Using tongs, coat eggplant slices in flour, then dip in egg mixture. Shake off excess.
Heat 1/4 inch oil in heavy large skillet over med-hi heat. Add eggplant in batches and cook till very lightly browned, approximately 2 minutes per side. Drain on paper towels.
Position rack in center of oven and preheat to 325 degrees F. (Steel knife) Mince spinach. Add reserved romano, remaining 1 egg, remaining 1/2 tsp. salt and ricotta cheese and blend till just combined, using 2-3 on-off turns. Spoon generous 2 tbsp. ricotta mixture onto short end of one eggplant slice. Roll up tightly. Repeat with remaining ricotta and eggplant. spread 1 cup tomato sauce in 9x13" non-aluminum baking dish. Arrange eggplant rolls seamside down on sauce. Top with remaining sauce. Sprinkle with mozzarella. (Can be prepared one day ahead.) Cover tightly and refrigerate. Bring to room temperature before baking. Bake 45 minutes. Serve hot.

Casseroles

Green Bean Casserole

2 cans whole green beans
3/4 cup brown sugar
1 lb. bacon (Oscar Mayer is
   best)
1/2 stick of melted butter
Salt, pepper, and garlic powder

Chris Hussey

Wrap bundles of green beans (appr. 8 beans) on 1/2 slice of bacon. Make glaze with melted butter, sugar, salt, pepper, and garlic powder and pour over beans in dish.

Bake at 375 degrees covered with foil for 45 minutes. Then uncover beans and bake for additional 10 minutes or so until browned.

Jaine Fricke

Casseroles

Green Chile Quiche

2 medium zucchini, shredded (squeeze
   excess water)
2 finely chopped green onions
1/4 cup chopped green chiles, canned
4 beaten egg whites
2 eggs or egg substitute
1 cup grated part skim mozzarella
1 cup grated cheddar cheese
1 1/2 cups evaporated skim milk
Vegetable coating spray

Saute squash and onion in a nonstick skillet over low heat until tender. Add water if squash begins to stick. Mix all ingredients and pour into 9 inch pan sprayed with vegetable coating spray. Bake at 350 degrees until firm and lightly browned. You may put into a pie crust if you wish.

Servings: 8

Casseroles

The Statler Brothers
(Johnny Fortune, Harold Reid, Don Reid, Phil Balsley)

Green Rice

1 lg. onion
1 stalk celery
  (Saute both onion and
   celery until clear and
   add to the following)
1 can cream of celery
   soup
1 can cream of mushroom
   soup
1 cup cooked rice
1 pkg. chopped broccoli
   (cooked)
1 small jar Cheese Whiz

Bake in greased baking dish for 25 minutes at 325 degrees.

The Statler Brothers pioneered the way for group performers in country music. When The Statlers started out, the prevailing wisdom was that groups simply could not make it in country music. The best professional advice was all negative. This was not what The Statlers' best instincts told them, however, so they did everything themselves--headlining, production, promotion -- up by their own bootstraps -- and success followed success after success.

Hal Ketchem

Hal Ketchem's Favorite Casserole

1 1/2 lbs. ground round
1/2 cup chopped onion
2- 8 oz. cans tomato sauce
1 tsp. sugar
1 tsp. salt
1 clove garlic, crushed
1/4 tsp. ground black pepper
1- 8 oz. pack cream cheese
3 cups noodles
1 cup sour cream
1/3 cup chopped green onion (use
    tops also)
1/4 cup chopped green pepper
3/4 cup grated mild cheddar cheese

Brown ground beef and onion. Drain. Stir in tomato sauce, sugar, salt, garlic and black pepper, simmer slowly, stirring often. Meanwhile, cook and drain noodles according to package directions. To the drained noodles, add sour cream, cream cheese, green onion and green pepper. Spread 1/2 the noodle mixture in a medium sized baking dish, cover with 1/2 meat mixture, layer with 1/2 the grated cheese. Continue this layering with remaining ingredients with grated cheese as last layer.
Bake 350 degrees for 30 minutes.

Casseroles

Meatball and Cabbage Caserole

MEATBALLS:
1 lb. lean ground beef
1 egg
1/4 cup milk
1/2 cup oats
1/2 cup finely chopped onion
1 tsp. salt
1 tbsp. Worchestershire Sauce

Larry & Margaret Fuda

Shred coarsley 1 medium head green cabbage, steam or par-boil 5 minutes. Drain. Place in 9x13" baking dish.

Pour milk over oats and let set for 5 minutes. Mix all meatball ingredients. Shape into 1 1/2" diameter meatballs. Place down in cabbage. Pour sauce over. Bake at 350 degrees for 1 hour 15 minutes.

SAUCE:
1 large (24 oz.) can diced tomatoes (can use stewed tomatoes)
1 6 oz. can tomato paste
2 tbsp. Worchestershire Sauce
2 tbsp. brown sugar
In large bowl, mix all ingredients.

HINT: If making smaller amount, use what you need of the tomato paste, and place the rest in plastic wrap and put in the freezer. You can slice off what you need for other recipes.

Megan Sheehan

Megan's Broccoli Rice Casserole

2 cups cooked rice (not instant)
1 pkg. chopped broccoli (thawed
   and drained)
1 8oz. jar Cheese Whiz
1 can cream of chicken soup
1 small can water chestnuts (cut
   fine)
3 tbsp. oleo
1/4 cup chopped onion
1/2 cup milk
1/2 cup chopped celery

Saute onion and celery in oleo. Mix all together, but only using 1/3 jar of Cheese Whiz. Put in casserole. Set remaining jar of Cheese Whiz in hot water to soften and be poured over top after baking. Bake at 350° uncovered for 40 minutes.

Serves 4 to 6.

Can be put together a day ahead and kept in refrigerator.

Casseroles

Mexican Coo

1 pkg. (10 count) tortillas
1 can cream of mushroom soup
1 can cream of chicken soup
1 can taco sauce (mild, med., or hot)
1 jar enchilada sauce
2 lbs. hamburger meat (brown)
1 small onion (brown with hamburger)
2 cups grated cheese (cheddar)

Megan Sheehan

Now you layer ingredients:
Tear 5 of the tortillas in pieces and place in bottom of casserole dish. Sprinkle 1/2 of the hamburger on and 1/2 of the enchilada sauce and 1/2 of the taco sauce then 1/2 of the cheese. Cover all with 1/2 of the two soups.

Repeat all the ingredients, ending once with the soups. Soup seals all the ingredients in.

Cook for 30 to 40 minutes at 350°.

William Lee and Brenda Golden
(The Oak Ridge Boys)

Casseroles

Mom's Chicken Casserole

Crust:
1 box Ritz Crackers (crushed)
1 1/2 sticks butter

Mix crackers and melted butter. Line the bottom of a casserole dish with the mixture, saving 1/4 of a cup for topping.

Filling:
1 can Cream of Mushroom Soup
1 can Cream of Chicken Soup
1 cup sour cream
1/2 cup water
1 clove of garlic
1 tsp. basil
pinch salt and pepper
1 can Water Chestnuts (chopped)
4 pieces chicken breast

Boil chicken breast and let cool. Pull apart meat in bite size portions. Spread chicken over crust. Sprinkle the chopped water chestnuts over chicken. In a bowl, mix the soups, sour cream and water together as well as the spices. Pour mixture over chicken. Top with left over crust. Bake at 325° until it is *golden* brown and bubbles.

Casseroles

Pineapple Casserole

1 large can pineapple chunks
   (drained) - save juice
1 1/2 cup grated cheddar cheese
   (Kraft)
3/4 cup sugar
3 tbsp. plain flour
1 stick oleo (melt)
1 sleeve Ritz crackers (crushed)
juice of pineapple

Lorrie Morgan

In a flat casserole (spray with pam).
Spread pineapple evenly - mix sugar and flour , with juice - pour over
pineapple - sprinkle with cheese, pour melted oleo over crushed crackers
and spread over top of pineapple and cheese. Bake 350° until hot and
lightly browned.

Allison Jordan

Pork Chop Casserole

4 pork chops
4 cups sliced potatoes
1 can cream of celery
    soup
1 cup milk
2 tbsp. onion, chopped
1/2 tsp. salt
1 1/4 tsp. pepper
grated American cheese

Brown pork chops on both sides. Place potatoes in 2 qt. baking dish. Mix remaining ingredients, except cheese; pour over potatoes. Place pork chops over potatoes; sprinkle with cheese. Bake at 375 degrees for 1 hour and 15 minutes.

Casseroles

Raymone's Beanie Weenies

1 medium size onion
1 medium size green bell
  pepper
2 celery sticks (10-inches each)
1/2 lb. ground beef
1 pkg. weiners
1 lg. can baked beans (55 oz.)
1 cup brown sugar
tabasco (15 dashes, or to taste)

Ray Stevens

Dice and saute the onion, green pepper and celery in butter until the onions look slightly opaque. Transfer this mixture to a large pot and set aside.

Crumble and brown ground beef, drain grease and transfer to the large pot also.

Drain baked beans, remove any pork fat and add to large pot.

Cut weiners into bite-size pieces and add to pot.

Stir in brown sugar.

Add tabasco.

Pour in casserole, bake at 350 degrees for 15 minutes.

Casseroles

Troy Beebe

Risto Alla Milanese (Lemon Risotto)

2 tbls. plus 2 teas. unsalted butter
2 tbls. olive oil
1/4 cup minced onion
1/4 tsp. saffron threads
1 1/2 cups Arborio rice, uncooked
4 3/4 cups <u>hot</u> chicken stock
1/4 cup plus 2 tsp. lemon juice
1/2 cup freshly grated Parmesan
    cheese

In a heavy saucepan over moderately low heat, melt 2 tablespoons of the butter and the olive oil. Add onion and lemon rind; saute slowly for 5 minutes. Add rice; stir to coat with oil. Turn up heat to high; toast rice, stirring, for 30 seconds. Immediately add 1/2 cup of the stock; reduce heat to medium-low and stir until stock is absorbed. Add more, 1/2 cup at a time, stirring constantly and adding more only when previous portion has been absorbed. When all stock is absorbed (about 20 to 25 minutes), stir in 1/4 cup of the lemon juice. The rice should be tender. If not, add warm water bit by bit until rice is tender yet firm.

Stir in Parmesan and remaining butter. Cook briefly to blend and melt cheese. Season to taste with salt and pepper. Serve immediately. Serves 4.

Casseroles

Spanish Rice And
Chicken Casserole

2-3 lbs. cut up chicken
1 tsp. garlic salt
1 tsp. celery salt
1 tsp. paprika
1 cup uncooked rice
3/4 cup chopped onion
3/4 cup chopped green pepper
1/4 cup minced parsley
1 1/2 cup chicken broth
1 cup chopped tomatoes
1 1/2 tsp. salt
1 1/2 tsp. chili powder

Ronnie Reeves

Place chicken in a greased 13 x 9 x 2 baking pan. Combine garlic salt, celery salt, and paprika. Sprinkle over chicken. Bake uncovered at 425 degrees for 20 minutes. Remove chicken from pan. Combine rice, onion, green pepper and parsley. Spoon into the pan. In a sauce pan, bring broth, tomatoes, salt and chili powder to a boil. Pour over rice, mixture, mix well. Place chicken pieces on top. Cover and bake for 45 minutes.

Casseroles

Squash Casserole

about 4-5 squash
1 white onion
2 tbsp. light olive oil
salt and pepper
mild cheddar cheese
regular or garlic croutons

Ty Herndon

This is real easy! Cup-up your squash, add the whole chopped onion, and salt and pepper to taste. (I like lots of pepper). Let this simmer in the oil, and cook until it's mushy. Take your casserole dish and layer the bottom with croutons. Then put a layer of grated cheese over the top of the croutons. Then pour the onion and squash mixture on top of the cheese and croutons. Now apply another layer of croutons and put the rest of the cheese on top. Put in the oven for thirty minutes at 300°.

Now, make some corn bread, and chow!

* My grandma taught me this recipe before I went off to work for Opryland (right out of high school).

Casseroles

Vegetable Casserole

4 tsp. margarine
4 tsp. flour
1 1/2 cup milk
1 can Veg-all
1 can asparagus (or use leftover
   vegetables)
1 tsp. lemon juice
1/2 tsp. salt
1/8 tsp. nutmeg
3 eggs, beaten
grated cheese or buttered bread crumbs

Hank Williams, Jr.

Melt margarine and add flour. Stir and cook until thick. Add milk slowly and stir and cook until thick. Add remaining ingredients and mix. Pour into a 2 quart casserole and top with cheese or bread crumbs.

Bake at 350 degrees for 30 to 40 minutes.

Notes

_____

_____

_____

_____

_____

_____

_____

_____

_____

_____

_____

_____

_____

_____

Chili

Chile Salsa & Huevos Rancheros 95
Chili Con Carne 96
Charlie's Diet Chili 97
Easy Chili 98
Green Chili 99
Hillbilly Chili 100
Hot & Spicy Chili 101
Mark's Special Chili 102
"Old Iron Pot" Family Style Chili 103
Otter Tail Chili 104
Sante Fe Chili 105
Skinny Chili 106

Chile Salsa & Huevos Rancheros

4 yellow Mexican peppers
3 tomatoes
4 cans Ortego chile salsa
8 eggs
1/4 cup oil
3 long green peppers
1/2 medium onion
1 cup Longhorn cheese, grated
8 corn tortillas
salt

Vikki Carr

Place about 3 tsp. (or just enough to cover bottom) of oil in a frying pan. Cut yellow and green peppers crosswise, in slices of about 1/4" across. Dice onions and cut the tomatoes; cover the pan, so that their juice falls into it, and saute until all ingredients have softened. Add 2 cups Ortego chile salsa; to make more sauce, add the remaining 2 cans of salsa. Let simmer 20 minutes. While the chile salsa is simmering, fry corn tortillas crisp in oil. Drain on paper, lightly salt top and place in oven to keep warm. Place a fried egg on each tortilla and spoon chile salsa over egg. Sprinkle with mild grated cheese. Garnish plate with avocadoes and refried beans.

Serves 4.

Glen Campbell

Chili Con Carne

3 lbs. chuck (ground)
3 onions
1 bell pepper
2 cloves garlic
1/2 tsp. oregano
1/4 tsp. cumin seed
2 small cans tomato paste
1 qt. water
salt
black pepper (ground)
3 tsp. chili powder
2- 17 oz. cans pinto beans

Brown chuck in iron kettle, add chopped onion and bell pepper, add crushed garlic, add oregano and cumin seed.

Add tomato paste, add water, salt and pepper, and chili powder.

Simmer for an hour and a half.

Add beans -- simmer half hour.

Let set two hours (or one week).

Charlie's Diet Chili

1 lb. lean ground beef
1 medium chopped onion
2 cups sliced celery
1/2 cup chopped green pepper
1/2 tsp. garlic salt
1 3/4 cups or 15 oz. can undrained
　kidney beans
4 cups or 2 lbs. cans undrained
　tomatoes
1 1/2 - 2 1/2 tsp. salt
1/2 - 1 tsp. chili powder
1 bay leaf

Charlie Daniels

Brown ground beef and onions in dutch oven. Thoroughly drain. Add remaining ingredients. Simmer covered 1-2 hours. Remove bay leaf. Serve hot. Freezes well.

8 servings
1 cup - 156 calories

Joe Nemechek

Easy Chili

1 lb. ground turkey meat
1 can Rotel tomatoes
1 8-10oz. tomato sauce
1 16 oz. can light red kidney
   beans
1 packet McCormicks Chili
   Mix
1 cup ketchup
Chili powder to taste

Brown turkey meat. Drain fat. In a separate pot combine all other ingredients. Add meat. Then cook on low heat for a few hours - uncovered. Serve with tortilla chips.

Green Chili

Pork shoulder roast - 3 to 4 lbs.
green chilies
garlic salt
1 can peeled whole tomatoes

Tanya Tucker

Cook pork shoulder roast in oven slow for 3 - 4 hours until done and can shred (roasting pan and some water).

When roast is done, take the juices from pan, skim off grease, put the pork juice and water in a pot (amount of water depends on how much soup you want).

Take fresh green chilies and dice on a plate. Sprinkle with garlic salt.

Then put in pot with shredded meat and water. Bring to a boil then simmer (the longer the better).

If the batch is hot from peppers, put a big can of peeled whole tomatoes and the juices in.

You can thicken with flour and water (like gravy) if you want it to be more like stew.

Aaron Tippin

Hillbilly Chili

4 cans pinto beans
4 cans crushed tomatoes
1 lb. lean ground beef
1 pkg. chili seasoning
1-2 tsp. vinegar
chili powder
jalapeno juice

Brown ground beef and drain off fat. Salt & pepper to taste. In a large pot combine ground beef, crushed tomatoes and pinto beans over medium heat. Add chili seasoning. Add chili powder and jalapeno juice to taste. Cover and let simmer for 30 minutes. Just before serving, add vinegar. This brings out the spices in the chili.

Hot & Spicy Chili

1 lb. ground beef
2 cans New Orleans style kidney
    beans, drained
2- 14 1/2 oz. cans stewed tomatoes
1 small can tomato paste
1- 12 oz. can Budweiser beer
1 lg. bell pepper chopped, coarse
1 medium white onion chopped, coarse
2 tbsp. hot chili powder
1/2 tsp. minced garlic
3 tbsp. yellow mustard
2 tbsp. sweet basil
1/2 tsp. oregano
2 jalapeno peppers, sliced
Lawery's hot 'n spicy seasoned salt to
    taste

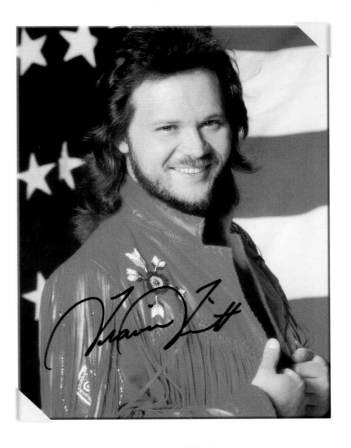

Travis Tritt

Brown ground beef, drain and transfer to crock pot. Add remaining ingredients and mix well. Cook on low 8 to 10 hours or high 3 to 4 hours.

Cover with your favorite shredded cheese and tabasco to taste and enjoy.

P.S. Have plenty of Pepto-Bismol on hand.

Mark Green and son Tyler

Mark's Special Chili

2 lbs. lean hamburger
1 1/2 packages of Durkee chili
   seasoning
1 15oz. can of diced tomatoes (I
   smash them, too)
1 8oz. can of tomato sauce
1/2 can of kidney beans (don't care
   for a lot of beans in my chili)
1 8oz. cup of water
1 small onion (diced)
1/2 small package of thin spaghetti
   (broken into thirds)
1/2 tsp. of salt
1/2 tsp. of pepper

Brown hamburger. Add onion, salt and pepper, and saute until tender. Drain and put in large pan. Stir in chili seasoning, diced tomatoes, tomato sauce, beans, and water.

In a separate pan, boil water and cook spaghetti until almost tender.

Add spaghetti to other ingredients. Bring to a boil. Reduce heat and simmer for 30-45 minutes. Watch carefully and stir occasionally. Add water only if necessary.

Makes 6-8 servings.

Chili

"Old Iron Pot"
Family Style Chili

5 lbs. Sirloin Steak
* 3 pkgs. McCormick's Chili
    Seasoning Mix
* Mexene Chili Powder
* Spice Island Chili Con Carne
    seasoning
* Cumin
* thyme
* sage leaves
* chopped raw onions
* chopped chili peppers
3-4 cans red kidney beans
3-4 cans whole tomatoes
1 can tomato paste
* garlic powder
* onion powder
2 tbsp. sugar
salt to taste

* Indicates that you must
    guess at the amounts
    to use. I never
    measure them.

Johnny Cash

Chop steak and cook until medium, with a little shortening added. Add packages of chili seasoning mix, cook for five minutes. Add beans, tomatoes, spices, raw onions, sugar, chili powder and/or chili con carne mix. Taste. (NOTE: If chili is too hot for the children, or the ladies, add one to two cans of tomatoes.) Add tomato paste. If chili seems too thick, add water. Simmer on LOW for twenty minutes. Serve with soda crackers, Pepsi, or Coke. This will serve twelve people, three helpings each!!

NOTES FROM JOHN:
This chili will be better tomorrow than today. IF properly taken care of overnight. I have also been known to substitute things, such as Snake meat, for the steak.

103

Mark Olson
(The Jayhawks)

Otter Tail Chili

1 lb. ground beef
1/2 lb. Jimmy Dean's pork
    sausage
1/2 lb. bacon
2 cans whole tomatoes
1 large onion
1 green pepper
1 red pepper
1 lb. fresh mushrooms
5 celery stalks
3 tbsp. chili powder
2 tbsp. cayenne pepper
1 tbsp. salt
1 tbsp. pepper
4 tbsp. tabasco sauce
1 can kidney beans
1 can chili beans

Fry ground beef, pork sausage, and bacon. In a large pot, mix the fried meat with whole tomatoes and simmer. Dice onion, green and red pepper, mushrooms, and celery and stir fry in pan. Mix with meat and tomatoes in pot. Add chili powder, cayenne pepper, salt, pepper, and tabasco sauce and cook for 1 hour on low. Add kidney and chili beans and cook for 45 minutes on low. Serve with sour cream and shredded cheddar cheese on the side.

Sante Fe Chili

pinto beans
ground sirloin beef
fresh green chilies
garlic
onion

Bellamy Brothers
(David and Howard)

Cook pinto beans in a crockpot until done. Fry ground beef in a frying pan, chop garlic and onion in the beef; then cook beef to taste.

Put whole fresh chilies into blender on medium, chop them until they're stringy.

Add chili and ground beef to pinto beans, then add salt to taste.

Serve in a bowl like soup, with jalepeno cornbread, and something cool to drink.

Skinny Chili

Tom T. Hall

2 lbs. ground beef
2- 6 oz. cans tomatoes
1- 6 oz. can tomato paste
1- 6 oz. can pimentos
3- 6 oz. cans red kidney beans
chili powder to taste
salt and pepper to taste
3 medium onions, chopped
3 stalks celery, chopped
3 green bell peppers, chopped

Brown ground beef in skillet, stirring until crumbly; drain; combine tomatoes, tomato paste, pimentos, beans and ground beef in stockpot; mix well. Simmer for 2 to 3 hours. Add chili powder, salt and pepper; mix well. Add onions, celery and green peppers. Cook for 20 minutes or longer or just until vegetables are tender-crisp for a crunchy texture. Serve with cornbread or crackers.

Yield: 8 servings

Cookies & Desserts

Cookies & Desserts

Banana Pudding 109

Best Chocolate Syrup Brownies 110

Brownies 111

Buck's Buttermilk Cobbler 112

Charlie's Cinnamon Sticks 113

Cherry Jubilee 114

Cowboy Cookies 115

Dad's Homemade Fudge 116

Grandma's Fudge 117

Ice Cream Delight 118

Mother Owens' Banana Pudding 119

My Sister Randy's Holiday Apple Chip 120

Peach Cobbler* 121

Pineapple Bake 122

Praline Cookie Crisps 123

Pumpkins Bars 124

Striped Delight 125

Sugar Cookies 126

Sweet Dreams Crunch 127

Cookies & Desserts

Banana Pudding

2- 12 oz. boxes vanilla wafers
  ('Nilla*wafers)
3 lbs. bananas, sliced
1 1/2 cups sugar
1/2 cup all-purpose flour
6 egg yolks
3 whole eggs
1/2 cup butter
dash salt
6 cups milk
2 tsp. vanilla

Dolly Parton

Layer sliced bananas and vanilla wafers in large baking pan. Mix together sugar, flour, eggs, butter and salt in heavy-bottomed saucepan. Add the milk, a little at a time. Cook slowly until the mixture thickens. Let it cool for a few minutes, then add the vanilla. Pour over bananas and vanilla wafers.

MERINGUE TOPPING:
6 egg whites
1 tsp. lemon juice
1 tsp. sugar
1 tsp. vanilla

Beat the 6 egg whites with lemon juice, sugar and vanilla until stiff. Spoon this mixture over the top of the pudding and brown at 350 degrees for 10 to 12 minutes or until golden on top. Makes 10 to 12 servings.

Cookies & Desserts

The Jordanaires
(Ray Walker, Duane West, Gordon Stoker, Neal Matthews)

Best Chocolate Syrup Brownies

1/2 cup butter
1 cup sugar
3 eggs
dash salt
1 cup all-purpose flour
3/4 cup chocolate-flavored
     syrup, canned
2 tsp. vanilla extract
3/4 chopped walnuts or
     pecans (pecans or
     walnuts, for garnish)

Preparation:
In a bowl, cream together butter, sugar and eggs until very creamy and well blended. Add salt. Stir in flour, mixing to blend well. Add chocolate syrup, vanilla and chopped nuts. Turn mixture into well greased and lightly floured 9 inch square pan. Smooth top. Bake at 350 degrees F. for about 35 minutes or until a toothpick inserted near center comes out clean. Cool in pan or wire rack but loosen cake at edges. Cut into squares. Garnish with pecan or walnut halves or dust with powdered sugar. This is quick and very tasty.

Cookies & Desserts

Trisha Yearwood

Brownies

2 oz. unsweetened chocolate
1/3 cup shortening
1 cup sugar
2 well-beaten eggs
2/3 cup plain flour
1/2 tsp. baking powder
1/2 tsp. salt
1 cup chopped pecans
1 tsp. vanilla

Melt the chocolate and shortening together. Add the sugar to the well-beaten eggs; combine the mixtures.

Sift flour with baking powder and salt.

Add the dry ingredients to the egg mixture; add nuts and vanilla.

Spread the dough evenly in a greased square pan, 8x8 by 2 inches. Bake at 350 degrees F. 25 to 30 minutes.

When cool cut into squares. These brownies keep well!

Red Steagall

Buck's Buttermilk Cobbler

1 cup flour
1 cup sugar
4 tbsp. Saco powdered
   buttermilk*
1/2 tsp. salt
1 tsp. cinnamon
1/2 tsp. nutmeg
1/4 tsp. soda
2 1/2 tsp. baking powder

Blend above well, then add 1 1/4 cups water and mix thoroughly, medium speed.

Pour into deep dish casserole in which 1 stick butter has melted, 4 cups fruit (peaches, apples, cherries, or berries). Pour over top. Bake in hot oven 350 degrees for 30 to 35 minutes. Serve with whipped cream, Cool Whip or plain.

* If using fresh buttermilk, 1 cup and 1/4 cup water.

Cookies & Desserts

Charlie's Cinnamon Sticks

Nonstick spray coating
1/3 cup margarine or butter
1 1/2 cups all-purpose flour
1/2 cup sugar
1/2 cup packed brown sugar
1 egg
1 tsp. ground cinnamon
1/2 tsp. vanilla
dash salt
1/2 cup finely chopped nuts

Charlie Chase
(Crook & Chase)

Line a 9x5x3 inch loaf pan with foil; spray with nonstick spray coating. Set aside.

Beat margarine or butter with an electric mixer for 30 seconds. Add about *half* of the flour, sugar, brown sugar, egg, cinnamon, vanilla and salt. Beat till thoroughly combined. Beat in remaining flour. Stir in nuts. Press evenly into prepared pan, using the back of a metal spoon to smooth surface. Cover; refrigerate overnight. Lift dough out of pan. Cut dough crosswise (parallel to the short sides) into 1/4-inch thick slices. Then cut entire dough block in half lengthwise, making two sticks from each slice. Place on a greased cookie sheet. Bake in a 375 degrees F. oven about 10 minutes. Makes 72 cookies.

Buckshot & Jina Jones

Cherry Jubilee

1 can of condensed milk
1 can of cherry pie filling
1 can crushed pineapple
  (drained)
1 medium tub of 'Cool
  Whip'

Option - Chopped pecans or shredded coconut may be added
to the batter if desired.

Mix all of the ingredients together in a bowl. Spread the batter
in a graham craker pie shell. Chill the dessert in the
refrigerator until you are ready to serve.

Cookies & Desserts

Cowboy Cookies

1 cup butter
1 cup brown sugar
1 cup white sugar
2 eggs
1 teaspoon vanilla
2 cups flour
1 teaspoon soda
1/2 teaspoon salt
1/2 teaspoon baking
    powder
2 cups rolled oats
1 small package semi-
    sweet chocolate chips
1/2 cup chopped nuts

Bill & Gail Davis

Cream sugars, butter, eggs, and vanilla until fluffy. Sift dry ingredients and stir in. Add oatmeal, chocolate chips and nuts. Drop by a teaspoonful on a cookie sheet. Bake at 350 degrees for 12 minutes. Makes 8 to 9 dozen.

Kenny Irwin, Jr.
(In Memory)

Dad's Homemade Fudge

2 tablespoons Butter
2 ounces Semi-sweet
    Chocolate
2 cups Sugar
2/3 cups Whole Milk
1 teaspoon Vanilla
1 cup Chopped Walnuts
    (optional)

Melt butter and chocolate in pan over medium heat. As soon as
it is melted, add sugar and milk. Cook, stirring often, until a
"soft ball" effect is achieved. Take off heat and let set for
twenty (20) minutes. After letting set, add vanilla and whisk
for 30 seconds. Adding nuts is optional. Pour fudge into a
9x9-in. pan and put into refrigerator for 3-4 hours. Cut into
squares. . .*or eat with a spoon like Kenny does - if your craving
is out of control and you just can't wait.*

Cookies & Desserts

Grandma's Fudge

4 cups sugar
1/4 tsp. (pinch) of salt
4 tbsp. of cocoa (slightly
   heaped)
3 tbsp. of dark karo syrup
2 cups milk (whole milk)

B.J. Thomas

Heat on low heat until boiling and will not separate in a cup of water.

Take off heat and add 3 tbsp. of butter.

Let set for 10 to 15 minutes.

Add 1 tbsp. of butter.

Whip until it thickens.

Pour in buttered plates.

Let harden.

Mario Gosselin

Ice Cream Delight

Crust Ingredients:
1 cup Graham Cracker crumbs
1 cup saltine cracker crumbs
1/2 cup margarine, melted

Filling Ingredients:
1 quart Butter Pecan Ice Cream, softened
2 3oz. packages Vanilla Instant Pudding
2 cups milk

Crust:
Mix together and pat in 9x13" pan. Bake at 350 degrees for 8 minutes. Set aside to cool.

Filling:
Mix with hand held mixer 2 minutes. Pour over cooled crust. Refrigerate until set, top with 8 oz. Cool Whip. Sprinkle with 2 crushed Skor Candy Bars.

TIPS:
Use chocolate Graham Crackers in crust as a change.
Cut large pieces of pecans into smaller pieces.
Use low fat milk, (1%) and Lite Cool Whip.
Freeze Skor Candy before crushing with a hammer.
Skor Candy Bars are similar to Heath Bars.

Cookies & Desserts

Mother Owens' Banana Pudding

1 cup sugar
3 tbsp. flour
1/2 tsp. salt
2 eggs
2 1/2 cups milk
2 tsp. vanilla
1 small box vanilla wafers
4 large bananas, sliced

Buck Owens

Combine sugar, flour and salt. Add eggs to milk and mix. Add to sugar/flour/salt mixture and blend. Cook over medium heat, stirring constantly, until thickened. Add vanilla and remove from heat. Line bottom of bowl or pan with vanilla wafers, then a layer of sliced bananas over the wafers. Put part of the cooked custard over the layers. Repeat another set of layers of wafers and bananas, ending with custard mixture. Sprinkle with wafer crumbs. Refrigerate until well chilled.

"This is one of my all-time favorites. When I was growing up in Texas, Mother would fix up big batches of this for all us kids and we liked it so much that somehow what leftovers there were never did stay in the icebox too long. When she used to fix it for me when I grew up, I got very greedy with it and sometimes I just refused to share with anyone."

"Mother cooked with 'dibs', 'fingerfuls' and 'just a bit's,' so these amounts are as close as anybody can come to a recipe. I hope you enjoy it as much as my family always had."

**My Sister Randy's
Holiday Apple Chip**

Lacy J. Dalton

- 1 1/2 dozen Granny Smith Apples - peeled, cored, sliced
- Sprinkle apples with sugar, cinnamon, flour to taste
- (Approximately 1 1/2 cups sugar, 1-1 1/2 tbsp. cinnamon, 4-6 tbsp. flour)
- Grease a *large* baking pan
- Add apple mixture - spread evenly 1 1/2 - 2 inches deep

- TOPPING:

3 cups flour	3 tsp. baking powder
1 cup white sugar	3 whole eggs *or* 1 whole w/2 whites
1/2 cup brown sugar	Dash of salt
cinnamon to taste (optional)	

- Cut to "crumb" consistency
- Sprinkle topping evenly over apple mixture
- Drizzle with 1-1 1/2 sticks melted butter or margarine
- Bake 350 degrees - 45-60 minutes or until crumb topping is lightly browned and apples are bubbling
- Cool 1/2 hour. Serve warm with ice cream or whipped cream. Also great the next morning for breakfast!

Cookies & Desserts

Peach Cobbler*

1 stick margarine
1 cup self rising flour (Bisquick preferred)
1 cup sugar
3/4 cup milk
2 cups sweetened peaches (1 large can sliced peached)

Jeff Burton

Step 1
Melt margarine in baking dish at 350 degrees
Step 2
Mix Bisquick, sugar, and milk
Step 3
Pour mixture over margarine (melted)
Step 4
Arrange sliced fruit on top of mixture, do not combine
Step 5
Bake unil top is golden brown

* This recipe was given to Mrs. Jeff Burton by Mrs. Betty C. Burton, Jeff's grandmother.

Chris Hussey

Pineapple Bake

2 cans tidbit pineapple
3/4 cup sugar
3 tbsp. pineapple juice
1 tbsp. flour
1 cup cheddar cheese, shredded
1/2 stick butter or margarine
1 package of Ritz crackers (1 insert)

Crumble crackers finely. Melt butter in skillet and add cracker crumbs and mix until smooth. Don't cook. Drain pineapple, reserving 3 tbsp. juice. Mix pineapple, juice, flour, cheese, and sugar in one bowl. Put this mixture in baking dish and pour cracker mixture over top.

Bake in 350 degree oven for 20 minutes.

Praline Cookie Crisps

Carter Family
(Anita, Helen, Carlene, June)

1 cup (2 sticks) butter
1 cup dark brown sugar
1 1/2 cups all-purpose flour
1 cup chopped pecans

Preheat the oven to 325 degrees.

Cream butter, adding sugar slowly; beat on medium speed until light. Stir in flour and pecans. The dough will be stiff and in a ball.

Divide dough into 6 equal pieces. Press out each piece into a 6-inch circle on a greased cookie sheet. Press the edges of each circle with the tines of a fork for decoration. Cut (not all the way through) the top of each circle as if you were cutting a pie in pieces.

Bake for 20 minutes. Cool on the baking sheets. The cookies break apart easily into wedges. Makes about 48 cookies.

Derrick Gilchrist

Pumpkins Bars

1 lb. (2 cups) solid pack pumpkin
1 cup oil
2 cups sugar
4 beaten eggs
2 cups flour
2 teaspoons baking powder
1/2 teaspoon salt
1 teaspoon soda
2 teaspoons cinnamon

Preheat oven to 350 degrees. Mix 1st four ingredients and then add the rest. Lightly grease cookie sheet pan and pour mixture into pan. Bake at 350 for 20 to 25 minutes, or until golden brown.

FROSTING
4 oz. soft cream cheese
1/4 cup soft margarine
1 teaspoon vanilla
1 3/4 cups powdered sugar

Mix all ingredients together and frost when cake is cool. Enjoy!

Cookies & Desserts

Striped Delight

1 1/2 cups Graham Cracker crumbs
1/4 cup sugar
1/3 cup melted butter
8oz. softened cream cheese
2 tablespoons of milk
1/4 cup sugar
8oz. Cool Whip
2 packages of 4 serving size pudding
3 1/2 cups cold milk

Darrell Waltrip

- Combine graham cracker crumbs, 1/4 cup sugar and melted butter. Press into 13 x 9 inch pan.
- Beat cream cheese with 1/4 cup of sugar and 2 tablespoons of milk until smooth.
- Fold in 1/2 of Cool Whip. Spread over crust.
- Prepare pudding as instructed on package using 3 1/2 cups of cold milk.
- Pour over cream cheese layer.
- Let stand in refrigerator over night.
- Spread remainder of Cool Whip.

Amy Grant

Sugar Cookies

2 cups self rising flour
1 cup sugar
1 cup Crisco
2 eggs
2 tsp. sweet milk

Combine 1 cup sugar and 1/2 cup Crisco, creaming well then add 2 eggs beaten, milk, mix well.
Drip by teaspoon onto a greased cookie sheet. Makes 5 1/2 doz.
Bake 375° for 10-12 minutes.
Sprinkle sugar on top.
If desired, add candried fruit, raisins, dates or nuts on top of each cookie.

Cookies & Desserts

Sweet Dreams Crunch

Reba McEntire

1 box white cake mix
1 stick butter
1 tsp. lemon juice
1 can cherry pie filling
1 9x9 square baking dish

Melt the stick of butter and pour directly into white cake mix. Mix until the mixture becomes doughy. Set aside.

Grease the baking dish with a small amount of oil.

Pour the cherry pie filling into the bottom of the dish and sprinkle the lemon juice over the cherries.

Crumble the dough "cake" mixture over the top of the cherry filling.

Bake at 325 degrees for approximately 1 hour or until golden brown. Let cool for 15 minutes before serving.

Notes

_____

_____

_____

_____

_____

_____

_____

_____

_____

_____

_____

_____

_____

_____

Meat

Meat

Beef N' Stout 131

Beefalo Rice Patty 132

Burrito Bake 133

Gilley's Fajitas 134

Grandma's Beef Stroganoff 135

Hamburger Stew 136

Hamburger-Vegetable Chowder 137

Hawaiian Meatballs 138

Hawaiian Pork Chops 139

Pheasant with Garlic 140

Pork Chops And Sauerkraut 141

Red Beans & Rice 142

Saltimbocca (Veal Scallops with Prosciutto & Sage) 143

Sloppy Joes 144

Southwest Beef & Bell Pepper Stew 145

Sterling's Favorite Pork Chops 147

Stuffed Doves 148

Sweet and Tangy Meatballs 149

Teriyaki Burgers 150

Meat

Beef N' Stout

1 tbsp. butter
1 tbsp. of corn oil
2 lbs. of top round steak
   cut into two inch
   cubes
4 medium sliced onions
2 cups halved mushroom
   buttons
2 tbsp. of flour
1/4 cup stout (dark beer)
1 bay leaf
1 tsp. dark brown sugar
salt and pepper to taste

Gene Johnson
(Diamond Rio)

Heat butter and oil in large dutch oven and cook meat for 10 minutes or until meat is brown.

Remove meat from pot with slotted spoon.

Add onions and mushrooms and fry for 5 minutes or until they are softened.

Season with salt and pepper to taste. Add flour and stir well so flour absorbs fat.

Return the meat to the pan and pour in the stout. Add the bay leaf and brown sugar. Stir well to mix.

Cover and cook gently on the stovetop on low heat or place into the oven at 300° for two and a half hours. Make sure the meat is tender. Serves 4-6.

**Serve with hot crusty german rye bread and sauted carrots and zuchini sticks.

131

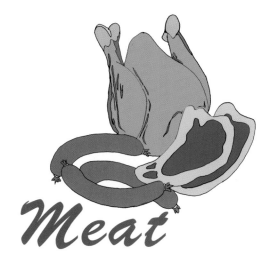

Meat

Ricky Van Shelton

Beefalo Rice Patty

Beefalo (or any prime or lean beef)
Onion
Olive oil
Black pepper
Parsley
Green bell pepper
Wickers Barbeque Marinade
Corn starch
Water
Tomato wedges
Rice
Beef bouillon cubes

Saute strips of beefalo and onion in olive oil. Add black pepper to taste. To 1/2 cup Wicker's Barbeque Marinade & Baste, add 1 tbsp. parsley and 1/4 green bell pepper. Baste beefalo with mixture.

In another pan, cream 1 tbsp. corn starch in 1/3 cup of water. Add to beefalo mixture. Let beefalo simmer; add tomato wedges and simmer for 5 minutes more.

Meanwhile, cook rice with beef bouillon cube added to the water. Serve beefalo over rice.

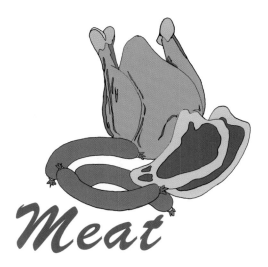

Meat

Burrito Bake

8 - 10 large flour tortillas
1 lb. ground beef - cooked and
   drained
1 can refried beans
1 can green chilies
1 can sliced black olives
1 cup green onions, chopped
1 large jar of medium or mild salsa
8oz. sour cream
Shredded mild cheddar cheese

Tony Stewart

Oven: 350 degrees

Fill tortillas with first five ingredients, fold and place in greased 9 x 13 pan. Cover burritos with sour cream and cheddar cheese. Bake for 10 - 15 minutes or until cheese is melted.

Serve hot with salsa, lettuce and tomatoes. Enjoy!!

Mickey Gilley

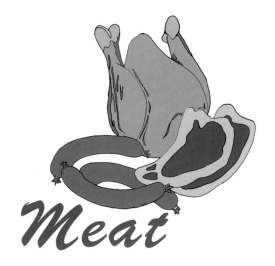

Gilley's Fajitas

16 oz. choice skirt meat
1 pkg. Gilley's Mesquite Marinade
2 large bell peppers
1 medium red bell pepper
1 medium yellow onion
2 cups shredded lettuce
2 cups grated cheddar and Jack
   cheese
2 cups Pica de Gallo
12- 6" flour tortillas
1/2 lime

Have skirt meat cleaned and tenderized. Marinade beef according to instructions on the back of Gilley's Mesquite Marinade package. Julienne cut bell peppers and onions. Charbroil or saute beef and cut into strips. Saute onions and bell peppers. Serve on a sizzling hot platter. Squeeze fresh lime over beef, bell peppers and onions to finish. Serve shredded lettuce, cheese blend and Pica de Gallo on the side.

Heat and slightly brown tortillas and serve on the side.

Enjoy!!!

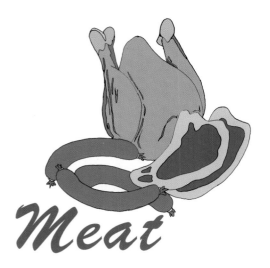

Meat

Grandma's Beef Stroganoff

1 can Cream of Mushroom
   soup
1 lb. cubed beef
8 oz. pkg. sour cream
1 box Minute Rice
corn starch

Jody Lynn

Place beef cubes in 3 quart pot and add enough water to cover. Bring to a boil then cover and reduce to medium heat. Cook beef until tender - approx. 3 - 4 hours. Add Cream of Mushroom soup and 3 more cups of water. Heat until soup dissolves. Meanwhile, combine cornstarch with enough water to make creamy paste. Gradually add this mixture to beef mixture, stirring constantly. Allow to simmer 5 minutes. Prepare Minute Rice as directed. Add sour cream to beef mixture and stir until dissolved - DO NOT BOIL.

To serve, pour beef mixture over rice.

Approximate cooking and preparation time: 5 hours

Serves 6

Mel Tillis

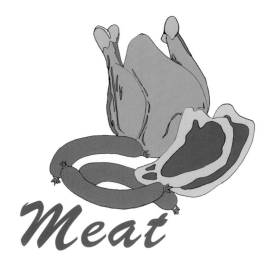

Hamburger Stew

2 lbs. ground beef
4-5 large carrots
3-4 large potatoes
1 large onion
1 pkg. frozen chopped okra or 9-10
    fresh pods
salt
pepper

Brown beef in skillet, drain off excess grease. Put ground beef in large pot.

Add:
Chopped onion
Potatoes - cut in cubes
Carrots - sliced thin
Salt and pepper to taste

Cover ingredients with water and cook with lid on for 30 minutes. Add okra - cover and cook an additional 15 minutes. You may have to add water while cooking. Serve over rice.

Yields: 6 servings

Meat

Hamburger-Vegetable Chowder

1 lb. lean ground beef
3 tbsp. butter or oil
2 cups canned tomatoes (1- 14 oz.
   can with juice)
2 medium carrots diced
1/2 cup diced celery
1 medium onion chopped
2 tsp. salt
1/4 tsp. pepper
1 1/2 quarts water
1/3 cup rice, regular long grain

Wynonna Judd

Brown hamburger in oil over medium heat. Then, add all other ingredients except rice. Cook on low for one hour, then add rice.

Cook until rice is done; add more water or tomato juice if it is too thick. V8 juice may be substituted for liquid.

Makes 6 servings.

Faith Hill

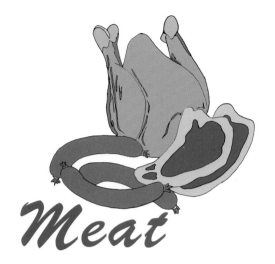

Hawaiian Meatballs

1 1/2 lbs. lean ground beef
1 cup soft bread crumbs
1 tbls. onion, minced
1/4 tsp. salt
1/8 tsp. cloves
1/2 tsp. ground ginger
1 egg
1 can (20 oz) crushed pineapple, drain but
     reserve syrup
1/3 cup lemon juice
1/3 cup firmly packed light brown sugar
2 tbls. soy sauce
1/2 cup beef boullion
2 tbls. cornstarch
1 green pepper, seeded and chopped, opt.

In large bowl, combine beef, crumbs, onion, spices, egg and 1/4 cup drained, crushed pineapple. Mix well. Shape into 1" meatballs. Brown meatballs, then drain all fat. Add enough water to pineapple syrup to create 1 cup. Combine pineapple, syrup, and all remaining ingredients in sauce pan and stir just until sugar is melted. Add to cooked meatballs and bake at 350 degrees for 25 - 30 minutes. Good served over rice.

Hawaiian Pork Chops

4-8 pork chops
4 oz. sliced water chestnuts
4 oz. sliced bamboo shoots
4-6 sliced, fresh mushrooms
1 small can drained, chunky pineapple
1 reg. size jar sweet & sour sauce
Minute Rice - amount depending upon
    number serving

Irlene Mandrell

Fry pork chops in just enough oil to brown them. Once cooked, remove from pan and set aside.

Combine water chestnuts, bamboo shoots and mushrooms in pan and cook on medium until brown. (Amount of mushrooms depends upon personal taste).

Add drained pineapple to mixture in pan and cook for approximately one minute, stirring constantly.

Blend in one jar of your favorite sweet and sour sauce.

Return pork chops to pan, let sauce and chops simmer on low.

Prepare rice according to package directions. Put pork chops and sauce on top of bed of rice. Serve.

Hank Thompson

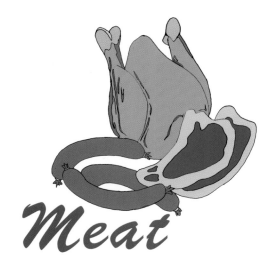

Pheasant with Garlic

30 garlic cloves, (yes 30) peeled (from about 4 heads)
1 stick (1/4 lb) unsalted butter
1 medium shallot, minced
6 chicken livers
2 pheasants
1 tbs. Cognac or Brandy
salt and pepper to taste
1 cup chicken stock or canned broth
8 slices French bread (about 1/2 inch thick), toasted, with crusts removed
Watercress, for garnish

In large saucepan of boiling water, blanch the garlic cloves for 3 min.: then drain. Preheat oven to 450°. In a small saucepan, melt 2 tablespoons of butter over moderately high heat. Add the shallot, chicken livers, and pheasant livers and saute for 2 minutes, until livers are just pink inside. In a blender or food processor, combine the liver mixture, the Cognac, salt and pepper and process until smooth. Set aside. Season the pheasant inside and out with salt and pepper. In a large ovenproof skillet, melt the remaining 6 tablespoons butter over moderately high heat. Add the pheasant and saute, turning, for a total of 9 minutes - 3 minutes on each side and 3 min. on the back. Distribute the garlic cloves over the pheasants and roast in the oven for 15 minutes, turning the garlic cloves after 5 minutes so that they do not burn. Remove the skillet from the oven. Transfer the pheasants and garlic to a warmed platter and cover with foil to keep warm. Preheat the broiler.

Meanwhile, make the sauce. Pour off the excess fat from the skillet. Add the stock and bring to a boil over high heat, scraping up any brown bits from the bottom. Boil until the mixture is reduced to a syrupy glaze, about 5 minutes. Season with salt and pepper to taste.

Working quickly, spread the liver paste on the toasted French bread slices. Place on a baking sheet and run under the preheated broiler for 1 minute.

To serve, arrange 4 croutons on each of 2 warmed plates. Cut the pheasants in half and place next to the croutons. Garnish with the garlic cloves and watercress. Spoon the sauce over the pheasants.

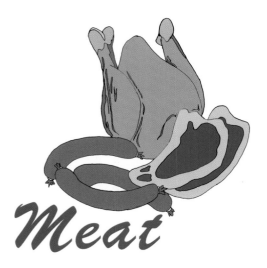

Meat

**Pork Chops
And
Sauerkraut**

4 butterfly pork chops
1/4 cup butter
1/2 small onion, chopped
Cavender's seasoning mix
1 jar Vlasic sauerkraut

Ronnie Dunn
(Brooks & Dunn)

Season pork chops generously with Cavender's and pepper. Saute pork chops and onion together until brown. Add sauerkraut (partially drain liquid), and simmer for one to two hours. Serve with mashed potatoes and vegetables of your choice.

Ronnie Gene Dunn grew up playing in his father's band in west Texas. He played in clubs in Texas and Oklahoma for years until he won the Marlboro Talent Search and soon got the attention of Arista label head, Tim DuBois.

Kix Brooks
(Brooks & Dunn)

2 lb. dried red kidney beans
1/2 lb. salt pork
6 fist-sized ham hocks (or more)
15" pepperoni sliced & quartered
    in 3/4" chunks
Hot Italian sausage links (remove
    casing and brown separately -
    these will break up in the long
    cooking process, but the flavor
    is terrific!
Kielbasa 3-10" lengths
Smoked beef sausage 3-10"
    lengths

Meat

Red Beans & Rice

3-4 3" onions diced (2 cups or more)
4 stalks celery, sliced diagonally
1 1/2 - 2 cups diced green peppers
1 1/2 - 2 cups diced red bell peppers
2 or 3 fresh tomatoes sliced
2 lg. cans whole peeled tomatoes, put
    in the juice from only one can
1 bunch green onions chopped
1 lg. can tomato sauce
4-6 pods garlic (if you use powder,
    cover the whole top with a layer)
3 tbsp. tabasco (or more)
1/2 tsp. thyme
3 tbsp. Worcestershire sauce
1 tsp. crushed red pepper
3 tbsp. cumin
1/2 tbsp. oregano (or more)
1 tsp. pepper
1 tbsp. salt

I add most of these to taste, so it's hard to determine precise amounts.
All during the cooking, I taste and add more of this and that.

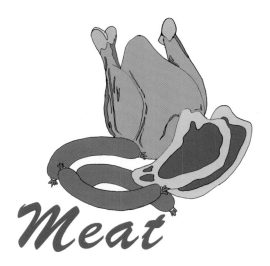

Meat

Saltimbocca
(Veal Scallops
with Prosciutto
& Sage)

1 1/4 lbs. leg of veal, cut into 12
    scallops
Salt and freshly ground black pepper
12 fresh sage leaves
12 paper-thin slices prosciutto
2 tbls. unsalted butter
3 tbls. dry white wine
1 1/2 tbls. minced parsley

Troy Beebe

Place each scallop between pieces of oiled waxed paper and, using a mallet or the bottom of a skillet, pound to a uniform 1/8-inch thickness. Salt and pepper scallops lightly. Put a sage leaf on each and cover with a slice of prosciutto. Secure prosciutto to scallop with toothpicks.

Melt 1 tablespoon of the butter in each of two large skillets. Add scallops and brown quickly on both sides. When scallops are just barely cooked, transfer them to a warmed serving platter; remove toothpicks. Scrape juices and browned bits from one skillet to the other. Add the wine to the skillet with the juices and reduce slightly over high heat. Pour sauce over scallops; garnish with parsley.

Serves 4.

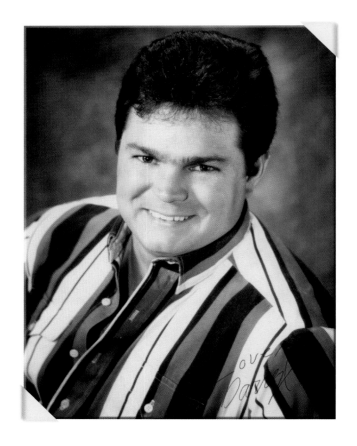

Darryl Wayne

Sloppy Joes

2 lbs. ground round
2 large onions
Kraft hickory smoked
   bar-b-q sauce

Brown ground round in a pot, add onions, salt &
pepper and bar-b-q sauce. Cook on low til
onions are clear and meat and sauce has cooked
down. Serve on hamburger buns.

Darryl was born on Dec. 2 in Inglewood, Calif., but his parents moved back to
Louisiana when Darryl was two months old. He performed on stage at Twitty City
daily. He loves good country music, boating, scuba diving, and karate. He is also a
train enthusiast.

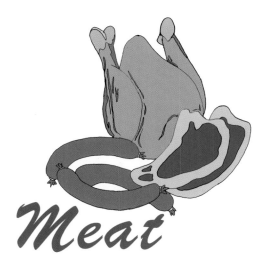

Southwest Beef & Bell Pepper Stew

1 cup dried pinto beans, rinsed, picked
    over
2 3/4 lb. boneless chuck roast, well
    trimmed and cut into 1 1/2 inch
    pieces
salt and pepper
3 tbsp. flour
8 garlic cloves, minced
1 1/2 cups red Zinfandel wine
1 28oz. can Italian plum tomatoes, drained
1/2 tsp. dried red pepper flakes
2 bell peppers, red and/or yellow cut into
    1 1/2 inch triangles
6 tbsp. vegetable oil
2 large onions, cut into 1/2 inch pieces
1 jalapeno chili, minced with seeds
3 tbsp. tomato paste
2 cups beef stock or canned low-salt broth
    (can use chicken)
1 smoked ham hock
11oz. kielbasa sausage, cut diagonally into
    1 inch wide pieces

Pat Seavers
(Pirates of the Mississippi)

2 poblano chilies
    (a fresh green chili, sometimes
    called a fresh pasilla, available at
    Latin American Markets and some
    supermarkets)
3 zucchini, cut into 1 inch thick
    rounds
Crusty bread
Santa Fe Seasoning*

(Continued on the next page)

145

Southwest Beef & Bell Pepper Stew

from Pat Seavers

(Pirates of the Mississippi)

(Continued from the previous page)

Place beans in heavy medium saucepan with enough cold water to cover. Bring to boil. Remove from ehat. Cover and let stand 1 hour. Drain beans. Place beef in large bowl. Season with salt and pepper. Sprinkle 2 teaspoons Santa Fe Seasoning over; toss well. Add flour and toss to coat.Heat 4 tablespoons oil in heavy 4 quart Dutch oven over medium high heat. Add meat in batches and brown well. Transfer to bowl using slotted spoon. Add remaining 2 tablespoons of oil. Reduce heat to medium. Add onions and all but 2 teaspoons remaining seasoning mix and toss to coat. Add garlic, jalapeno and tomato paste and stir 1 minute. Add wine and bring to boil, scraping up browned bits. Add both stocks, tomatoes, ham hock and red pepper flakes and bring to simmer. Return meat to Duch oven. Reduce heat, cover partially and simmer 30 minutes, stirring occasionally. Add beans, cover partially and simmer 1 hour. zUncover, add reserved 2 teaspoons seasoning mix and simmer until meat and beans are tender, stirring occasionally, about 45 minutes. Degrese stew if necessary. Remove ham hock; trim fat and discard. Cut ham meat into 1/2 inch pieces. Mix into stew. (Stew can be prepared 1 day ahead simply cover and refrigerate at this point. Bring to simmer before continuing with recipe.) Cook kielbasa in heavy large skillet over medium heat until cooked through, about 2 minutes per each side. Transfer to plate. Add peppers, poblano chilies and zucchini and saute until crisp-tender, about 5 minutes. Mix sausage and vegetable into stew and simmer unti ljust tender, about 5 minutes.
Ladle into bowls. Serve with crusty bread.

*Santa Fe Seasoning

1/4 tsp. cinnamon	3 1/2 tsp. ground cumin	2 /12 tsp. chili powder
2 tsp. dried thyme, crumbled	1/4 tsp. ground allspice	2 1/2 tsp. ground coriander
2 tsp. dried oregano, crumbled	1/4 tsp. ground cloves	1/4 tsp. cinnamon

Mix all ingredients in bowl. (Can be made 1 week ahead. Store airtight.)

Meat

Sterling's Favorite Pork Chops

6 pork chops
mustard
1 cup flour
salt
pepper
seasoned salt
1 can cream of mushroom soup
milk

Sterling Marlin

Spread both sides of chops with mustard. Mix flour and seasonings. Coat chops well and brown in oil. Put in a sprayed dish, add cream of mushroom soup and 1 can of milk. Bake for 1 hour at 350°.

This is real easy and Sterling loves it!

Meat

Hank Thompson

Stuffed Doves

1 lb. port sausage
1 chopped onion
1/2 to 1 tsp. sage
1 clove garlic, minced
10 dove breasts
1/4 cup cooking oil
1 cup stock or water
salt, pepper and cayenne to taste

Brown sausage. Add chopped onion and minced garlic; cook until limp, but not too brown. Add salt, pepper and cayenne. Cook until sausage is well done. Drain off fat. Set aside.

In heavy pot, brown doves in hot oil. Stuff doves with sausage mixture. Season with salt and pepper, add beef or chicken stock or water. Cover and simmer for about 1 hour or until doves are tender. Add more liquid if necessary.

* Serves 4 to 6

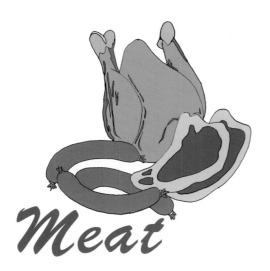

Meat

Sweet and Tangy Meatballs

Bill Elliott

Meatballs:
2 lbs. ground chuck
1 egg
1 large onion minced
(may use dry minced onions)
1 1/2 tsp. salt

Sweet and Tangy Sauce:
1-10oz. jar grape jelly
1-12 oz. bottle chili sauce
3 tbsp. lemon juice

Mix ground beef, egg, and salt together. Shape into 1" meatballs. Cook until brown at 350°. Remove from pan and drain.

Combine chili sauce, jelly, and lemon juice. Cook over medium heat, stirring constantly until jelly melts. Add meatballs to sauce, simmer 10-15 minutes.

**If using for a party remove to chafing dish to keep warm and serve.

Kim Forester
(Forester Sisters)

Teriyaki Burgers

1 1/2 lb. ground beef
1 tbsp. soy sauce
1 tbsp. honey
1 clove garlic, crushed
1/2 tsp. salt
1/4 tsp. ground ginger

Shape meat into patties. Combine remaining ingredients in a small bowl, stirring well; brush on patties. Place patties on lightly greased rack of a broiler pan; broil 4 inches from heat about 15 minutes on each side or until desired degree of doneness.

Pasta

College Noodles 153

Fettuccine Primavera 154

Ham Sauce and Tortellini 155

John Michael's Favorite Homemade Egg Dumplings 156

Kipp and Zel's Lasagna 157

Lasagna 158

Pasta Primavera 159

Pierogy 160

College Noodles

1 large Vidalia or sweet onion
   chopped
1/4 lb. butter (1 stick)
1 tsp. salt
1 tsp. pepper
1 lb. elbow macaroni #35 (1 small
   box)
1 lb. container cottage cheese

Blaise Alexander

Saute onions in butter; add salt and pepper to taste. Boil macaroni as directed on box. Drain off macaroni and add sauteed onions in butter, mix well. Add the cottage cheese and stir through as you serve the noodles.

Ward Burton

Fettuccine Primavera

1 cup sliced mushrooms
1/2 cup sliced onions
1 clove of minced garlic
2 tbsp. butter
8 oz. cream cheese
1 medium tomato chopped
1/4 cup milk
1/4 cup Parmesan cheese
1 tsp. Italian seasoning
4 oz. cooked spinach fettuccine
4 oz. cooked plain fettuccine

Cook mushrooms, onions, garlic, and butter in a large skillet.
Add remaining ingredients expect fettuccine: mix well. Cook
until mixture begins to boil stirring constantly. Add fettuccine.
Lower heat and simmer for 5 minutes.

Pasta

Ham Sauce and Tortellini

6 tbsp. butter
1 small diced onion
3 tbsp. flour
2 tsp. minced garlic (garlic powder will substitute)
1- 4 oz. can of drained mushrooms
12 oz. sliced or diced ham (deli slices work also)
1 cup heavy whipping cream
10 oz. milk
1/2 cup of parmesan cheese
1 cup frozen peas
pinch of salt and pepper
tortellini (cheese filled)

Dana Williams
(Diamond Rio)

Saute onion, garlic and 3 tbsp. of butter; add ham and brown slightly - push to the side of the pan. Melt second half of butter. Add flour, salt and pepper - stir till smooth. Add mushrooms and stir. Add milk and cream and stir till sauce thickens. Add cheese, peas, simmer for twenty minutes. Stir occasionally.

Tortellini: Bring water to a boil and add the tortellini. Bring the water to a boil once again. Cook till the tortellini floats. Drain. Pour the sauce over the cooked tortellini and serve.

Serves two with leftovers.

John Michael Montgomery

John Michael's Favorite Homemade Egg Dumplings

2 cups plain flour
2 eggs
2 tbsp. vegetable shortening
1 cup chicken broth - cooled to
   room temp.
1/2 to 1 cup of cold water

Mix flour, eggs, melted shortening, salt and chicken broth together to make dough adding enough cold water to make a stiff dough. Knead several times. Roll out dough as thin as possible. Cut into strips 2 inches wide. Cut into strips 4 to 6 inch strips. Drop dumplings into boiling broth. Boil until dumpling cuts easy with a fork, approximately 15 to 20 minutes, stirring often so they will not stick.

Kipp and Zel's Lasagna

1 pkg. "no boil" lasagna noodles
   (about 9-12 noodles)
1 lb. ground beef
1 8oz. can tomato sauce
1 pkg. American Cheese Singles
1 tsp. salt
1 tsp. garlic salt
pinch of oregano
pinch of parsley

Mila Mason

Preheat oven to 350°. In large saucepan brown ground beef. Drain. Stir in tomato sauce. Add salts, parsley, and oregano. Stir gently and let simmer on low. Layer lasagna noodles on bottom of large casserole dish. Pour beef sauce over noodles. Top with 3-6 slices of cheese. Repeat steps 5-7 until dish is near full. Sprinkle with parmesan cheese and bake until cheese is browned - about 30 minutes.

* Tastes best when served surrounded by thick slices of garlic bread.

Pasta

Johnny Benson

Lasagna

1 lb. ground beef
chopped onion
Chopped green peppers

Sauce Mixture:
16 oz. tomato sauce
6 oz. tomato paste
2 cups water
1/4 cup sugar
1/2 tsp. garlic
1/2 tsp. Italian seasoning
1 1/2 tsp. oregano
9 lasagne noodles

Top:
1 cup Mozzarella

Cheese Mixture:
1 small container cottage cheese
1 small container Ricotta cheese
1 cup Parmesan cheese
1 egg
1 large square cream cheese
2 cups Mozzarella cheese

Cook lasagne noodles and let cool. Brown ground beef, onion, and green peppers. Add all sauce ingredients and simmer, uncovered, for 30 minutes.

Cream egg and cream cheese in mixer. Stir in cottage cheese, Ricotta cheese, Parmesan cheese, and Mozzarella cheese.

In 9"x13" pan, layer sauce, noodles, sauce, and cheese. Use 3 layers of noodles and top with 1 cup Mozzarella cheese. Bake at 350° for 45 minutes.

Pasta Primavera

1/2 lb. box of thin spaghetti, cooked
    according to package directions
1/2 pound broccoli*
2 tbsp. olive oil
2 cloves garlic, peeled and crushed
1/2 lb. young zucchini,*washed and
    thinly sliced
1/2 lb. mushrooms, sliced
1 1/2 tsp. dried basil
1/2 tsp. salt
1/2 tsp. coarsely ground pepper
2 tbsp. water
2 tbsp. grated Parmesan cheese

Mark Collie

While spaghetti is cooking, wash broccoli and cook it in a small amount of boiling water until crisp but tender. Meanwhile, heat 1 tbsp. olive oil in a large frying pan and sautegarlic 3 minutes; add zucchini and cook until slightly browned. Add mushrooms; cook until mushrooms are tender. Drain broccoli; slice into bite-sized pieces and add it to zucchini and mushrooms. Stir in seasonings. When spaghetti is "al dente" stop cooking by pouring cold water into pot; drain spaghetti. Return it to the pot, stir in 2 tablespoons of water, remaining 1 tablespoon olive oil, Parmesan cheese, and vegetable mixture. Cover and reheat over low heat.

*You may substitute eggplant, red or green sweet peppers, green beans, onions or other vegetables in season.

6 servings (yield: 6 1/4 cups)

Michelle Wright

Pierogy

Dough:
1 egg
1 tbsp. sugar
1 cup milk
1 cup hot water
3 tbsp. oil
1 tsp. salt
4 1/2 cups four

Stuffing:
4 potatoes
1 small onion (finely chopped)
2 bacon slices (finely chopped)
salt and pepper to taste
1 cup grated cheddar cheese
boiling pot of water

Dough:
Wisk ingredients (except flour and water) together adding hot water slowly. Add flour until dough mixture does not stick. Mix well with your hands. Ball dough into a thin layer. Cut into 3 inch squares.

Stuffing:
Cook potatoes and keep warm. Fry onion and bacon. Combine remaining ingredients to potatoes along with onion and bacon. Begin to boil water. Spoon potato mixture into a dough square. Fold dough square to form a triangle. Press edges together to seal (may need to dab water around the edges to make dough stick). Once you have added all of the potato mixture into dough squares, put into boiling water (3 or 4 at a time). Wait until they come back to surface of water (they first sink) and boil for one minute. Take out of boiling water, brush with oil or butter so they don't stick together. You can stop here or brown in oven turning over once. Garnish with any combination: salt, pepper, chili sauce, sour cream, chives, fried onions, or salsa (salsa is not too Polish, but very hip!)

Pies

Pies

Apple Stack Pie 163

Aunt Becka's Not So Sweet Pecan Pie 164

Cherry Cheese Pie 165

Double Layer Pumpkin Pie 166

Japanese Fruit Pie 167

John Michael's Favorite Pumpkin Pie 168

Million Dollar Pie 169

Open-Face Peach Pie 170

Pecan Pie 171

Apple Stack Pie

6 cups self-rising flour
1/2 tsp. baking soda
1 cup butter
4 eggs, beaten
1/2 cup molasses
1 cup sugar
1 tsp. vanilla
1 tsp. cinnamon
2/3 cup milk

Dolly Parton

Sift together flour and soda; add butter and mix well. Beat together eggs, molasses, sugar, vanilla, cinnamon and milk. Add flour mixture and mix until it looks like bread dough. Turn onto a floured board or cloth and knead for a few seconds. Divide the dough into six equal layers, and roll out into thin layers like pie crust. Grease flour six round cake or pie pans. Put one layer into each pan and pat flat. Bake for 10 to 15 minutes at 300 degrees. Remove from pans and cool.

FILLING:

1 lb. apples - peeled, cored and sliced
1/2 cup water
1/2 cup sugar
1/4 tsp. cinnamon
1/8 tsp. allspice filling

Cook apples slowly in water until soft. Strain. To each cup of pulp, add 1/2 cup sugar and cinnamon and allspice. Cook over low heat until sugar is dissolved, and until mixture is thick. Place filling between layers, and stack one layer on top of the other. This recipe will make two 3-layer cakes or one 6-layer cake. This cake is best after it sits for 2 or 3 days. Makes 10 to 12 servings.

Hut Stricklin

Aunt Becka's Not So Sweet Pecan Pie

1/4 cup butter or margarine
1/2 cup sugar
1 cup lite corn syrup
1/4 tsp. salt
1 tsp. vanilla
3 eggs
1 cup pecans
1 - 9" unbaked pie shell

Cream butter to soften. Add sugar and cream till fluffy. Add syrup, salt, vanilla - beat well. Add eggs one at a time beating well after each addition. Stir in pecans & pour into pie shell. Bake at 350 degrees for 15 minutes then lower temp. to 325 degrees for 30 minutes or until knife inserted comes out clean.

Cherry Cheese Pie

1- 9 inch graham cracker crunc crust
   (bought or your own recipe for
   crumb crust)
1- 8 oz. pkg. cream cheese, softened
1- 14 oz. can sweetened condensed
   milk
1/3 cup lemon juice
1 tsp. vanilla extract
1- 21 oz. can cherry pie filling,
   chilled

June Forester
(Forester Sisters)

In large mixer bowl, beat cheese until fluffy. Gradually beat in
sweetened condensed milk until smooth. Stir in lemon juice and
vanilla. Pour into crust. Chill 3 hours or until set. Top with desired
amount of pie filling before serving. Refrigerate.

Randy LaJoie

Double Layer Pumpkin Pie

1 - 3 oz. cream cheese (softened)
1 cup plus 1 tbsp. Cold Milk or Half
   & Half
1 tbsp. sugar
1 1/2 cup Cool Whip Topping
1 Graham Cracker Pie Crust
2 small pkgs. vanilla instant pudding
1 - 16 oz. can pumpkin
1 tsp. ground cinnamon
1/2 tsp. ground ginger
1/4 tsp. ground cloves

Mix: Softened cream cheese with 1 tbsp. of milk or half & half, and sugar. Mix with wire whisk until smooth. Gently stir in whipped topping. Spread on bottom of graham cracker crust.

Pour 1 cup of milk or half & half into mixing bowl. Add instant pudding mix. Beat with wire whisk until blended well. Let set for about 3 minutes.

Stir in pumpkin and spices. Mix well. Spread over cream cheese layer. Chill in refrigerator for at least 2 hours.

If desired, top with whipped topping and crushed nuts. Serves 8.

Japanese Fruit Pie

2 eggs, separated
1 cup sugar
1/2 cup butter, melted
1 tbsp. vinegar
1/2 cup coconut
1/2 cup pecans
1/2 cup white raisins
1 9-inch pie crust
whipped cream, optional

Patty Loveless

Combine egg yolks, sugar, butter, and vinegar. Add coconut, pecans, and raisins. Beat egg whites until stiff. Fold into other mixture. Pour into pie crust. Bake at 325 degrees 50 to 60 minutes. Cool. Top with whipped cream.

Yield: one 9 inch pie.

John Michael Montgomery

John Michael's Favorite Pumpkin Pie

1 unbaked pastry shell
2 cups pumpkin (not canned)
1 cup light brown sugar
2 eggs well-beaten
1/2 tsp. salt
1/4 cup evaporated milk
2 tbsp. margarine melted
2 tbsp. dark cooking molasses
1 1/2 tsp. pie spice or 1/4 tsp.
   nutmeg
1/4 tsp. ginger
1 tsp. cinnamon

Heat oven to 450 degrees. Combine pumpkin, sugar, eggs, salt, evaporated milk, margarine, molasses and spices. Put into pie shell after all of the ingredients have been well blended. Bake at 450 degrees for 10 minutes and reduce heat to 350 degrees and bake for 30 minutes with the oven door ajar. Pie is done when inserted knife comes out clean.

Pies

Jennifer McCarter
(McCarter Sisters)

Million Dollar Pie

1 can Eagle Brand
    sweetened condensed
    milk
1/4 cup lemon juice
small can flake coconut
3/4 cup chopped pecans
1 lg. can crushed
    pineapple, drained
1 lg. whipped topping,
    thawed

Mix all of the above together and put into graham cracker crust.
Refrigerate. Makes 2 big pies.

The McCarters are from Sevierville, Tennessee, and were known to perform on the county courthouse steps. The girls were often teased in high school for their love of country mucic and dancing. They moved from their hometown to pursue their dreams in Nashville. In 1987, the girls' initial single was number five on the national charts, turning their dreams into reality.

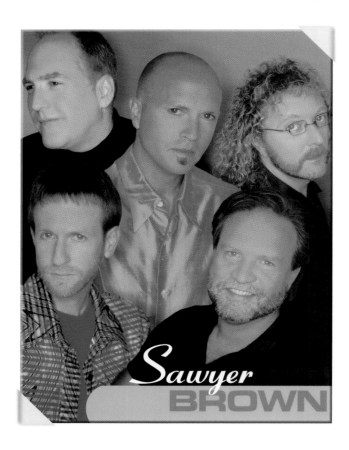

Sawyer Brown
(Duncan Cameron, Mark Miller, Joe Smyth, Gregg Hubbard and Jim Scholten)

Open-Face Peach Pie

1 unbaked 9-in. pie shell
2- No. 2 1/2 cans peach
   halves
1 egg
1/2 cup white sugar
2 tbsp. cream
1/4 cup brown sugar
1/4 cup butter
1/4 cup flour

Line unbaked pie shell with drained peach halves. Beat together egg, white sugar and cream - pour over peaches. Mix like pie crust brown sugar, butter and flour. Sprinkle on top of peaches. Bake 20 minutes in 375 degree oven, then 30 minutes longer in 350 degree oven.

Yield 6 servings.

Pecan Pie

3 eggs
1 cup white sugar
1 cup dark corn syrup
1 cup whole pecans
1/8 tsp. salt
1 tsp. vanilla extract
1 unbaked 9-inch pie shell

Billy Ray Cyrus

Beat eggs, sugar, and corn syrup together. Add pecans, salt, and vanilla. Pour into unbaked pie shell. Bake at 425 degrees for 10 minutes, then reduce heat to 350 degrees and complete baking in 25 to 30 minutes. Brush melted butter or margarine over pecans while pie is hot. Serve slightly warm or cold.

Notes

Poultry

Poultry

Boxley Style Chicken 175
Chicken Barbecue 176
Chicken Breast In Sour Cream 177
Chicken Breasts And Veggies 178
Chicken Breasts Diane 179
Chicken Corn Chowder 180
Chicken Enchiladas 181
Chicken Fried Steak 182
Chicken Marsala 183
Chicken Mozzarella 184
Chicken Pan Pie 186
Chicken Stir Fry 187
Chicken With Tortillas 188
Chinese Chicken Wings 189
Crispy Chicken with Lemon Sauce 190
Fete Di Pollo Con Pignoli E Limone (Chicken Steaks) 191
Grilled Chicken & Pasta 192
Grilled Chicken Breasts 193
Indonesian Chicken 194
Italian Style Chicken 195
Quick Chicken Creole 196
Quick-Fry Chicken & Vegetables 197
Thai Chicken & Noodles 198
Turkey Smoked Sausage Jambalaya 199

Poultry

The Statler Brothers
*(Johnny Fortune, Harold Reid,
Don Reid, Phil Balsley)*

Boxley Style Chicken

8-10 chicken breasts
   (boned and skinless)
2 pkgs. dried beef
1 lb. of bacon
1- 10 3/4 oz. can of
   cream of mushroom
   soup
1- 8 oz. container of sour
   cream

Preheat oven to 300 degrees. Cover bottom of large baking
dish with dried beef. Wrap bacon around chicken breasts;
then place wrapped chicken on top of dried beef in casserole
dish. Mix soup and sour cream together until smooth and
spread on top of chicken breast. Place in oven and bake for
2 1/2 hours.

Makes 8-10 servings.

175

Poultry

Chicken Barbecue

This is a wonderful recipe that the local fire departments and churches use when they have chicken barbecue fund-raisers. They'll fix 500 or more chicken halves to sell to raise money. This is my favorite chicken recipe.

Rick Mast

Barbecue Sauce

Item	5 halves	10 halves	50 halves
Oil	1/4 pint	1/2 pint	2 1/2 pints
Vinegar	1 cup	1 pint	2 1/2 quarts
Salt	2 Tbls.	4 Tbls.	1 1/2 cups
Pepper	1/2 tsp.	1 tsp.	5 tsp.
Poultry seasoning	1 tsp.	2 tsp.	2 1/2 Tbls.
Garlic (minced)	1/2 clove	1 clove	5 cloves

Cooking time is 1 1/2 to 2 hours. . .don't burn. Baste chicken halves every five to seven minutes. It's best if the chicken is marinated in the sauce for 8 to 12 hours. I marinate overnight. I grill it on low heat and baste it frequently and only turn it twice.

Poultry

Chicken Breast In Sour Cream

4 tbsp. flour
1/2 pint sour cream
1 can cream of mushroom soup
1 cup milk
Pepper
Garlic salt
4 Chicken breasts

Buckshot Jones

Mix flour with sour cream. Combine with all other ingredients except chicken. Place chicken breasts in baking dish and pour mixture over them. Bake at 350 degrees for 1 1/2 hours.

Serves 4.

*Great served with mashed potatoes.

George Jones

Chicken Breasts
And Veggies

chicken breasts
chopped carrots
chopped celery
chopped onions
canned or frozen whole
   kernel corn
canned or frozen English
   peas
chopped potatoes
garlic powder to taste
chicken bouillon

Combine chicken breasts, carrots, celery, onions, corn, peas, potatoes, garlic powder and bouillon in large Dutch oven; mix well. Add enough water to cover. Bake at 300 degrees for 2 hours, stirring occasionally. Serve with hot corn bread.

Poultry

Chicken Breasts Diane

Kevin LaPage

For 4 servings you will need:
4 large boneless chicken breast halves or 8
   small
1/2 tsp. salt
1/4 to 1/2 tsp. black pepper
2 Tbsp. olive or salad oil
2 Tbsp. butter or margarine
Juice of 1/2 lime *or* lemon
2 Tbsp. brandy *or* cognac, optional
3 Tbsp. chopped fresh chives *or* green onions
3 Tbsp. chopped parsley
2 tsp. Dijon-style mustard
1/4 cup chicken broth

Preparation time: 20 minutes

1.   Place chicken breast halves between sheets of waxed paper or plastic wrap. Pound slightly with mallet. Sprinkle with salt and black pepper.
2.   Heat 1 tablespoon each of oil and butter in large skillet.
3.   Cook chicken over high heat for 2 minutes on each side. Do not cook longer or they will be overcooked and dry. Transfer to warm serving platter.
4.   Add chives *or* green onion, lime juice and brandy, if used, parsley and mustard to pan. Cook 15 seconds, whisking constantly.
5.   Whisk in broth. Stir until sauce is smooth. Whisk in remaining butter and oil.
6.   Pour sauce over chicken. Serve immediately.
Tips: You can pound chicken breasts flat and leave flattened between sheets of plastic wrap. Wrap them airtight in one package and freeze for later use.
Good served with: Noodles with tomato sauce, steamed broccoli and a fresh salad.

Mike Dillon

Chicken Corn Chowder

6 Slices bacon
1 Medium onion
3 tbsp. all purpose flour
3 cups chicken broth
4 medium potatoes diced
1 teas. dried sage
1/4 teas. pepper
2 cups chopped cooked chicken
2 cups milk
1 10oz. bag frozen whole kernel corn

In dutch oven, cook bacon over med/high heat. Remove bacon and set aside. Add onion to bacon drippings, cook until tender. Stir in flour until smooth and bubbly (1 minute). Stir in chicken broth, potatoes, sage, and pepper. Cover and cook 15 to 20 minutes or until potatoes are tender. Add remaining ingredients except bacon. Cook until heated through. Top each serving with bacon. Enjoy!

Poultry

Chicken Enchiladas

5- 4 oz. skinned, boned chicken breast
    halves
vegetable cooking spray
1 small chopped onion
3 tbsp. chopped fresh cilantro
1 jalapeno pepper, seeded and chopped
    (or to taste)
3- 10 oz. cans enchilada sauce, divided
8- 6 inch corn tortillas
1 pkg. 8 oz. low fat sharp cheddar
    cheese
one bunch green onions, chopped
1/3 cup vegetable oil (optional)

Sweethearts of the Rodeo
(Janis Gill, Kristine Arnold)

Cover chicken with water in a medium saucepan. Cook over medium heat 20 minutes, or until tender. Drain and cool. Shred chicken and set aside.

Coat a non-stick skillet with cooking spray; place over medium heat. Add onion, cilantro, and jalepeno pepper. Saute until tender. Add 1 can enchilada sauce and chicken. Cook 10 minutes.

Soften tortillas by wrapping in aluminum foil and baking at 350 degrees for 5 minutes. Fill each tortilla with chicken mixture and 1 tbsp. green onions; roll up, and place seam side down in a 13x9x2 inch baking pan. Heat remaining 2 cans enchilada sauce; pour over enchiladas. Top with cheese and green onion. Bake at 350 degrees for 30 minutes.

Willie Nelson

Chicken Fried Steak

2 lbs. tenderized beef cutlets

Dip into:
2 eggs (beaten)
3 tbsp. milk
1 tsp. salt
1 tsp. pepper
1/2 cup flour
Alternate dipping cutlets into egg
    mixture and flour.

Deep fry in a skillet until golden brown. Drain cutlets on a paper towel.

WHITE GRAVY
Pour off all grease used to fry cutlets except to 1/3 cup. Add about 1/8 cup of flour to grease, stir until mixture looks like a rue. Add more flour if necessary. As the rue thickens and starts to bubble, add 2 cups of milk. Let mixture simmer stirring constantly until gravy is thick. If gravy gets too thick, add more milk and stir. Salt and pepper to taste. Willie likes a lot of pepper.

Serve cutlets smothered in white gravy, add several fresh vegetables, green onions, sliced tomatoes and cornbread and you've got a meal.

Poultry

Chicken Marsala

1/2 cup chicken broth
2 tsp. cornstarch
1 tsp. lemon juice
1/4 tsp. dried oregano, crushed
1/4 tsp. dried basil, crushed
1/4 tsp. pepper
1/8 tsp. salt
1 tbsp. cooking oil
1 clove garlic, minced
3/4 cup sliced mushrooms
1 cup sweet red, yellow and/or green pepper strips
1/4 cup sliced green onion
3 medium skinned and boned chicken breast
    halves, cut into thin bite-size strips (9 ozs.)
2 tbsp. dry Marsala *or* dry sherry
Hot cooked pasta

Lorianne Crook
(Crook & Chase)

For sauce, combine chicken broth, cornstarch, lemon juice, oregano, basil, pepper and salt. Set aside.

Add oil to a large skillet. Preheat over medium-high heat. Stir-fry garlic in hot oil for 15 seconds. Add mushrooms, sweet pepper and onion. Stir fry for 2 to 3 minutes or till vegetables are crisp-tender. Remove vegetables. Add more oil, if necessary.

Add chicken to skillet. Stir-fry 2 to 3 minutes or till done. Push chicken from center of skillet. Stir sauce; add to center of skillet. Cook and stir till bubbly. Return all vegetables to skillet. Cook and stir til heated through. Remove from heat. Stir in Marsala. Serve over pasta. Serves 2 to 3.

Poultry

Chicken Mozzarella

Steve Wariner

2 cups tender-cooked spaghetti (no oil or salt added during cooking)
low-calorie cooking spray
1 lb. chicken breast meat, cut into bite-sized pieces
3/4 cup tomato sauce
1 cup thinly sliced fresh mushrooms
1/4 cup finely chopped yellow onion
1/4 tsp. garlic powder
1/4 tsp. dried basil leaves
1/2 tsp. dried oregano leaves
1/4 tsp. freshly ground black pepper
1/8 tsp. fennel seeds
1/2 tsp. low-sodium Worcestershire Sauce
2 tbsp. chopped fresh parsley
1-2 tbsp. dry red wine
1/2 cup (2 ozs.) shredded mozzarella cheese
1 tbsp. freshly grated Parmesan cheese

Preheat oven to 350 degrees F.

Rinse spaghetti in cold water and drain well. Spread in bottom of a 8-inch square baking dish coated with a low-calorie cooking spray. Flatten chicken breast to 1/4 inch thickness and place on top of spaghetti.

(continued on next page)

184

Poultry

Steve Wariner

(Chicken Mozzarella continued)

In mixing bowl, combine tomato sauce and mushrooms, bell pepper, onion, garlic powder, basil, oregano, black pepper, fennel seeds, Worcestershire sauce, parsley, and wine. Mix well and spoon over chicken and spaghetti.

Bake uncovered, for 30 minutes. Top with mozzarella cheese and bake 8-10 minutes longer, or until cheese melts. Sprinkle with Parmesan cheese.

MAKE AHEAD DIRECTIONS

To Freeze: Complete steps 2-3 of the recipe, using an 8 inch square foil pan in place of the baking dish. Wrap tightly with freezer foil, and freeze. You can keep this for up to one month.

To Serve: Let mixture thaw completely. Preheat oven to 350 degrees F. Place wrapped container in oven and bake for 40-45 minutes or until chicken is tender. Top with mozzarella cheese and bake 8-10 minutes longer, or until cheese melts. Sprinkle with Parmesan cheese AND ENJOY!

Loy Allen Jr.

Chicken Pan Pie

2 lbs. boneless, skinless chicken
   breast
2 cans mixed vegetables
1 can cream of chicken soup
1 can chicken broth

Topping:
1 cup flour
1 cup buttermilk
1 stick melted butter
dash of pepper

Cook chicken. Cut into bite-size pieces. Mix vegetables, soup, broth, and chicken in large baking dish. Heat until bubbly at 425°. Mix topping while dish is heating to bubbly. Spoon topping on dish. Bake for 30 minutes or until crust is browned.

Chicken Stir Fry

1/2 lb. chicken tenders
stir fry sauce
2 bell peppers
bag of sliced almonds
1 can of water chestnuts
1 tsp. of canola oil
celery
broccoli
carrots
1 onion

Doug Stone

First, brown chicken tenders (add a dash of salt and pepper),
add 1/4 cup of water. Add the veggies and steam thoroughly.
(You can add as many veggies or as few as your heart desires.)

Serve on a bed of Uncle Ben's converted rice.

Poultry

Mark Smith

Chicken With Tortillas

8 chicken breasts
6 corn tortillas
1 can chili salsa
1 can chili without beans
1/2 c. onions
1 can cream of celery or mushroom
    soup
1/2 lb. grated cheddar cheese
1/2 lb. grated Monterey Jack cheese

Boil breasts until tender (reserve broth), break into bit size pieces. Put into 13x9" pan. Break tortillas into bite size, put over chicken, chopped onions over that. Combine soup, chili, salsa and one cup chicken broth until blended. Pour over chicken, sprinkle cheese over top. Serve with hot salsa, sour cream and ripe olives. Bake at 350 degrees for 1 hour.

Poultry

Chinese Chicken Wings

5 lbs. chicken wings
1/2 cup sugar
1 cup packed brown sugar (dark)
1 cup soy sauce

Trace Burton

Disjoint wings into 3 pieces, discard tips. Place in shallow baking dish. Combine soy sauce, sugar and brown sugar in bowl and mix well. Pour over chicken. Bake 30 minutes, at 325 degrees, turn chicken and bake 35 minutes. Turn chicken once more and bake 15 minutes longer. Serve hot.

Suzy Bogguss

Crispy Chicken
with Lemon Sauce

4 skinless/boneless breast halves
1/2 cup flour
2 tsp. black pepper
1/2 tsp. salt
1 tbsp. olive oil
1/2 cup lemon juice
1/4 cup sugar
1/4 cup chicken stock
2 tbsp. soy sauce
2 tsp. lemon zest
2 tsp. cornstarch

Mix together flour, salt, and pepper. Dredge chicken. Preheat sauce pan for one minute. Add oil. Cook chicken 5 minutes on each side. Remove - keep warm. Mix together lemon juice, sugar, stock, soy sauce, lemon zest, and cornstarch. Add to pan and allow to thicken. Cover chicken breasts with sauce and serve.

Poultry

Fete Di Pollo Con Pignoli E Limone (Chicken Steaks)

4 whole chicken breasts, split and boned
3 cups chicken stock
1 cup dry white wine
1/2 cup minced carrot
1/2 cup minced onion
2 tbls. white wine vinegar
Pinch hot red-papper flakes
Grated rind of 1 lemon
Salt
3 tbls. butter
3 tbls. olive oil
1/4 cup toasted and finely ground pine
    nuts
2 tbls. lemon juice

Troy Beebe

2 tbls. minced Italian parsley
2 tbls. toasted pine nuts, for garnish

Pound chicken breasts between two pieces of oiled waxed paper to 1/4-inch thickness. Put stock, wine, carrot, onion, vinegar, pepper flakes, and lemon rind in a nonaluminum saucepan and bring to a boil. Simmer uncovered until sauce is reduced to about 2 cups (about 1 hour). Strain through a sieve; taste and add salt if necessary.

Heat two large skillets over moderately high heat. Divide butter and oil between them; when butter foams, add chicken and saute quickly, about 45 to 60 seconds per side. Remove chicken to a warm serving platter and keep in a warm oven while you finish the sauce.

Bring chicken stock mixture to a boil and whisk in ground pine nuts, lemon juice, and 1 tablespoon parsley. Pour sauce over chicken and garnish with whole pine nuts and remaining parsley. Serves 8.

Mike Skinner

Grilled Chicken & Pasta

chicken breasts
seasoned garden dressing mix
oil
balsamic vinegar
spiral pasta
red wine Vinagrette dressing
Kraft fat-free ranch dressing

- Marinade 6 chicken breasts for 8 hours in dressing
    (SeasonedGarden dressing mix, added to oil and balsamic vinegar)
- Grill the chicken for about 25 minutes, turning every five minutes
- Serve with spiral pasta, boiled for 12 minutes
- Red Wine Vinagrette dressing served over the pasta
- Kraft fat-free ranch dressing for dipping the chicken
- Water to drink

Poultry

Grilled Chicken Breasts

4 halved skinless breasts
2 tsp. Dijon mustard
1/4 tsp. black pepper
1/3 cup margarine
2 tsp. lemon juice
1/2 tsp. garlic salt
1 tsp. whole dried tarragon

Mark Martin

Preparation
- Spread mustard on both sides of chicken and sprinkle with pepper. Cover and refrigerate 2 - 4 hours.
- Melt margarine, stir in lemon juice, garlic salt and tarragon. Cook over low heat for 5 minutes, stirring occasionally.
- Place chicken on grill, baste with sauce. Turn and baste until done.

Yields 4 servings.

Poultry

Billy Thomas
(McBride & The Ride)

Indonesian Chicken

1 1/2 lbs. boneless
   chicken
Marinade:
1 clove garlic
2 tbsp. soy sauce
1 tbsp. oil
1 tsp. cumin
1 tsp. coriander

Cut chicken into 3/4 inch cubes and mix with marinade. Chill for two hours. Put about 5-6 pieces of chicken on skewers and grill about 4 inches about coals until done. Baste often with 3 tbsp. lemon juice; 2 tbsp. soy sauce; 1/4 tbsp. cumin; and 1/4 tbsp. coriander.

PEANUT SAUCE FOR DIPPING
1 cup water
2/3 cup peanut butter
2 cloves garlic

Heat it until boils and thickens. Remove from heat. Mix in 2 tbsp. brown sugar, 1 1/2 tbsp. lemon juice, 1 tbsp. soy sauce and 1/4 tsp. red pepper or red crushed dried chilies. Serve over rice.

Poultry

Italian Style Chicken

1 lb. chicken cutlets
1 egg
3 tablespoons milk
1/2 cup flour
1 cup Italian Style bread crumbs
*Marinara Sauce
1 lb. grated mozzarella
*If you need to add extra
  ingredients, do so*

Debbie Gibson

MARINARA SAUCE RECIPE
1 large can of crushed tomatoes
3 or 4 cloves of crushed garlic to taste
3 tablespoons olive oil

Brown garlic in olive oil, add tomatoes plus 1/2 can of water, cook over low heat about 1 hour (add more water if necessary) season to taste, salt, pepper, a little hot pepper. Prepare chicken cutlets, beat egg and milk together, dip cutlets one at a time first in flour, egg thin breadcrumbs, fry in very hot oil remove and drain on paper towel, in a baking pan layer chicken cutlets, sauce and top with mozzarella cheese. Bake in 375 degree oven until cheese is melted.

Have fun and Good Luck!

Loretta Lynn

Quick Chicken Creole

3 tbsp. chicken fat
2 tbsp. chopped onion
1 minced clove garlic
3 tbsp. flour
1/4 tsp. salt
1/4 tsp. paprika
1/2 cup tomato puree or strained tomatoes
1 cup chicken broth
1 tsp. lemon juice
1/2 tsp. horseradish
2 cups diced cooked chicken meat
1/2 cup sliced fresh sauteed
 mushrooms

Melt the chicken fat and saute the onions and clove garlic. Stir in the flour, salt, and paprika. Add tomato puree or strained tomatoes and chicken broth and stir well. Stir and cook the following ingredients until they boil. Add lemon juice, horseradish, cooked chicken meat, sauteed mushroom and season to your choice of rice.

Poultry

Quick-Fry Chicken & Vegetables

1- 1 lb. boned and skinned chicken
    breasts, cut into 1/2 inch cubes
2 tbsp. vegetable oil
1 medium sized onion (chopped)
1 medium to large green pepper
1 tsp. salt
1/2 tsp. minced garlic
2 medium sized tomatoes, cut into
    chunks

Mark Herndon
(Alabama)

Heat oil in a medium skillet on medium heat until the oil is very hot. Add the chicken and stir until the chicken becomes golden brown. Add the remaining ingredients except the tomatoes. Cook for 5 to 8 minutes until the chicken is completely done. Add tomatoes and stir until they are warm. Serve over rice off by itself. Serve also with teriyaki sauce.

197

Teresa McCarter
(McCarter Sisters)

Poultry

Thai Chicken & Noodles

WHISK TOGETHER:
1/4 cup peanut butter
1 oz. toasted sesame seed
3 tbsp. each water, soy sauce,
   honey
1 tbsp. each sesame oil, rice vinegar,
   minced garlic
1 tsp. each minced ginger, red
   pepper flakes

TOSS WITH:
1 cup shredded chicken
1- 9 oz. pkg. angel hair pasta cooked
chopped fresh scallions

Can be served hot or chilled.

Poultry

Turkey Smoked Sausage Jambalaya

1/2 lb. smoked turkey sausage, sliced
1 tsp. corn oil
1 lg. onion, chopped
1 stalk celery
1 small sweet pepper (both chopped)
2 cloves garlic, sliced
2 tsp. tomato catsup
1 cup uncooked long grain rice
2 cup water
1 tsp. minced parsley
2 tsp. chopped green onion
salt and pepper to taste

Penny Gilley

Place sausage in pot with 1/2 cup water. Cook until water boils out. Remove sausage. Set aside. Add oil, saute onion and celery for 15 minutes. Add 1/4 cup water, sausage, sweet pepper, garlic and tomato catsup. Cook for 10 minutes. Stir in rice, fry for 2 to 3 minutes. Add water, parsley, green onion, salt and pepper. Let come to a boil, lower heat to simmer. Cook for 10 minutes covered. Stir and continue cooking covered for 15 minutes or until rice is tender. Serve 4.

Notes

_____

_____

_____

_____

_____

_____

_____

_____

_____

_____

_____

_____

_____

Salads

3 Bean Salad 203
7 Cup Salad 204
A Most Unusual Salad 205
Caesar Salad for Two 206
Chicken Salad a la Rogers 207
Curried Sprout Salad 208
Linguini Salad 209
Marty Roe's Mixed Picnic Salad 210
Megan's Mexican Salad 211
Pasta Salad 212
Quick Fruit Salad 213
Swinging Doors Pineapple Salad 214
Seven Layer Salad 215
Taco Salad 216

3 Bean Salad

1 pkg. (10 oz.) frozen lima beans
1 pkg. (10 oz.) frozen green peas
1 pkg. (10 oz.) frozen green beans
.

Bill Anderson

Cook on full boil for 20 minutes with salt added. Drain well.
Mix with sauce and serve.

SAUCE
1 1/2 cups mayonnaise
1 medium onion, chopped
1 1/4 tsp. Worcestershire sauce
3 hard boiled eggs, chopped

Barbara Mandrell

7 Cup Salad

1 cup grated coconut
1 cup cottage cheese
1 cup sour cream
1 cup chopped nuts
1 cup crushed pineapple
1 cup fruit cocktail
1 cup miniature marshmallows

Combine all the ingredients and refrigerate. This salad improves after it sits a day or two.

For over 30 years, Barbara Mandrell has received over 75 major awards, starred in her own top-rated variety show, and released over 30 albums that went to the top of the Country as well as the Pop charts.

A Most Unusual Salad

Gogi Grant

1/2 head iceberg lettuce, shredded
1 avocado, peeled and cubed
1 grapefruit, peeled and sectioned
2 tomatoes, peeled and quartered
3 tbsp. chopped chives
3 tbsp. lemon juice
salt and pepper to taste
1/3 cup butter

Combine lettuce, avocado, grapefruit, tomatoes and chives. Add lemon juice and salt and pepper. Heat butter until foamy and golden. Pour immediately over salad. Toss lightly and serve at once.

Serves 4.

Nikki Nelson
(Highway 101)

Caesar Salad for Two

1 clove garlic, pressed
1/4 tsp. anchovie paste
1/2 tsp. Grey Poupon
   mustard
3 dashes worcestershire
   sauce
3 dashes tobasco
1/2 lemon squeezed
1 tbls. egg beaters
1/4 cup olive oil
Parmesan Cheese -
   liberally mixed

Mix all these ingredients together. Toss with romain lettuce. Add croutons and fresh ground pepper.

Chicken Salad a la Rogers

2 cups cooked chicken (white meat)
3 dill pickles (non-kosher), skinned
1/2 cup chopped walnuts
1/4 cup slivered or chopped almonds

Kenny Rogers

Pick the chicken from the bone rather than cut it. Peel pickles with a potato peeler and chop. Mix all of the above ingredients lightly with mayonnaise of choice. You may prefer to add chopped scallions. Season to taste and serve on a bed of crisp lettuce.

Gogi Grant

Curried Sprout Salad

1 lb. bean sprouts
1 cup thinly sliced celery
3 tbls. chopped green onions
2 tsp. ground ginger
1 cup mayonnaise
3 tbls. soy sauce
2 tsp. curry powder
2 tsp. lemon juice
2 pkg. (3oz.) slivered almonds,
  toasted

Wash bean sprouts, dry thoroughly. Combine sprouts, celery, green onions and ginger. Set aside.
Combine mayonnaise, soy sauce, curry powder, and lemon juice for dressing. Pour dressing over vegetables and toss gently. Arrange on bed of lettuce and sprinkle with toasted almonds.
Serves 4.

* For one-dish meal, add 1 cup flaked tuna or cooked chicken.

Linguini Salad

1 lb. linguini
1 small onion
2 medium tomatoes
1 large cucumber
1 can medium pitted black olives
1 bottle McCormick Salad Supreme
1 bottle Seven Seas Viva Italian Salad
    Dressing - 16oz.

Peter Sospenzo

Boil linguini until tender. Drain and rinse with cold water. Dice onion and tomatoes into small pieces. Peel cucumber and dice into small pieces. Drain olives and chop in half. Add all vegetables to linguini in large bowl. Pour whole bottle of Salad Supreme over linguini and vegetables. Pour whole bottle of Italian dressing over linguini and vegetables. Mix well. Chill in refrigerator for one hour or more. Mix well before serving.

Marty Roe
(Diamond Rio)

Marty Roe's Mixed Picnic Salad

1 head of flowered broccoli
1/2 cup of raisins
1/2 cup of chopped onions
1/2 cup bacon bits (real or
    artificial)
2 shredded carrots

Mix all ingredients together well.

Dressing:
    1/2 cup sugar
    1/4 cup vinegar
    1 cup mayonnaise

Mix together well and pour over salad. Let chill and serve.

Megan's Mexican Salad

Megan Sheehan

1 head lettuce, shredded
1 lb cheddar cheese, shredded
1 (15 oz.) can red kidney beans,
    chilled, drained and rinsed
2 tomatoes, diced
1/2 onion, chopped
3/4 of (8oz.) bottle spicy-sweet
    French Dressing
1 (1/2 lb.) package corn chips,
    crushed

Combine all ingredients, except dressing and fritos.
Add dressing 30 minutes to 1 hour before serving.
Add corn chips just before serving. Toss to mix well.

Patty Loveless

Pasta Salad

3 cups broccoli florets
3 cups cauliflower florets
1/4 cup scallions
1 lb. package sliced turkey ham (cut
    into cubes)
1 5oz. jar spanish olives (sliced)
1 16oz. box Rotini Pasta
1 16oz. package feta cheese
1 tbls. parsley
2 tsp. ground pepper to taste
1/4 cup parmesan cheese
1 16oz. bottle of Paul Newman's
    Italian Dressing

Follow directions on the package for cooking pasta. Rinse with cold
water and set aside. Combine broccoli, cauliflower, scallions, turkey
ham and olives. Add cooked pasta and mix. Add feta cheese, parsley,
pepper and parmesan cheese and mix thoroughly. Shake and pour entire
bottle of Paul Newman's Italian Dressing and mix thoroughly. Chill and
serve. Makes a bunch.

Quick Fruit Salad

1 medium apple
1 medium orange
1 1/2 cup strawberries
1 cup seedless grapes
1 can fruit cocktail
1 cup coconut

Vern Gosdin

In mixing bowl, mix the apple, orange, strawberries and grapes. Pour the whole can of fruit cocktail with juice in mixing bowl. Add coconut. Mix well. You may use any fruit in season.

Vern grew up chopping cotton in Alabama and singing on the Gosdin Family Gospel Show on radio station WVOK in Birmingham, Alabama before leaving to form his own career.

Merle Haggard

Swinging Doors Pineapple Salad

1 pkg. lemon jello
1 small can crushed pineapple
  (drain and save liquid)
3 large bananas, sliced
1 cup miniature marshmallows
1/2 cup sugar
3 tbsp. flour
1 egg, well beaten
3 tbsp. butter
1 pkg. Dream Whip

Prepare jello as directed. Add drained pineapple, bananas, and marshmallows. Pour in square or small oblong pyrex dish. Let chill till firm. Then, add enough water to pineapple juice to make 1 cup. Add sugar, flour, beaten egg and butter to juice and cook until it thickens. Let cool, then fold in the whipped cream and spread over the gelatin. Garnish with chopped nuts.

(Guaranteed to keep the refrigerator doors swinging.)

Kathy Forester
(Forester Sisters)

Seven Layer Salad

lettuce, torn into bite-size pieces
1 pkg. frozen green peas,
    uncooked
1 medium red onion, thinly
    sliced and separated into
    rings
4 hard-boiled eggs, sliced
1 lb. bacon, cooked and
    crumbled
1 1/2 to 2 tbsp. sugar
1/2 to 1 cup mayonnaise
1 cup shredded cheddar cheese

Layer lettuce, peas, onion slices, egg slices and most of the crumbled bacon (save some for garnish). Sprinkle sugar onto the layers and cover with mayonnaise. Top with Cheddar cheese and garnish with remaining crumbled bacon. Refrigerate for at least 2 hours before serving. Store in covered container in refrigerator.

Kathy Forester
(Forester Sisters)

Taco Salad

1 lb. ground beef
1/2 envelope (1/4 cup) dry
    onion soup mix
3/4 cup water
1 medium head lettuce, torn in
    bite-size portions
1 lg. tomato, cut in wedges
1 small onion, thinly sliced
    and separated into rings
1/4 cup chopped green peppers
1/2 cup sliced green olives
4 oz. (1 cup) sharp natural
    cheddar cheese, shredded
1- 6 oz. pkg. corn chips

Brown beef in skillet; sprinkle soup mix over meat and stir in
water. Simmer, uncovered, for 10 minutes. In salad bowl,
combine lettuce, tomato, onion, green pepper, olives and
cheese, toss. Place lettuce mixture on individual salad plates.
Spoon on meat and top with corn chips. Serves 6.

Sauces & Soups

Blueberry Soup 219

Broccoli Cheese Soup 220

Gail's Best Bar-B-Q Sauce 221

Gumbo 222

Joe's Homemade Bean Soup 223

Lemon-Garlic Grilling Sauce 224

Mark Dufrense's Barbecue Sauce 225

Potato Soup 226

Raw Cranberry Sauce 227

Ricky's Chicken Pickin' Corn Soup 228

Soup Beans or Brown Beans 229

Spaghetti Sauce 230

Tomato Gravy 231

Tortilla Soup 232

Lisa Stewart

Blueberry Soup

2 cups fresh or frozen blueberries
  (set aside 1/4 cup for garnish)
1- 8 oz. can crushed pineapple, packed
  in water, not drained
1 tbsp. fresh lemon juice
1 cup pineapple juice
1/2 cup fresh mint leaves
3/4 cup plain yogurt
2 bananas
1 1/4 cup apple juice
Sprigs of fresh mint for garnish

Prep time: 5 minutes
Chill 2 hours

Combine 1 3/4 cup blueberries, pineapple, lemon juice, pineapple juice, mint leaves, 1/4 cup yogurt, 1 banana and 1 cup apple juice in food processor or blender. Puree until smooth. Pour into large bowl, cover and refrigerate at least 2 hours or overnight.

In food processor or blender, combine remaining yogurt, banana and apple juice. Puree until smooth. Cover and chill at least 2 hours or overnight.

Just before serving, separate into six chilled bowls. Float yogurt mixture on top and add mint garnish and remaining blueberries.

Tanya Tucker

Broccoli Cheese Soup

1 grated carrot
1 stalk celery
1 small onion
1 cup broccoli
2 cups grated cheese
2 cups chicken broth
4 tbsp. butter
1/3 cup flour
1/2 tsp. pepper
1 tsp. salt
2 cups milk

Combine broth, carrot, celery, onion, salt, pepper, and broccoli and cook until vegetables are tender. Make paste with the butter and flour. Add the milk to make a sauce. Add the sauce along with the cheese and vegetables mix and simmer until it thickens.

Sauces & Soups

Bill & Gail Davis

Gail's Best
Bar-B-Q Sauce

6 tablespoons catsup
2 tablespoons vinegar
2 tablespoons lemon juice
4 tablespoons Lea & Perrins
4 tablespoons water
4 tablespoons butter
6 tablespoons sugar
2 teaspoons salt
1 1/2 teaspoons chili powder
2 teaspoons paprika
2 teaspoons mustard
1/2 teaspoon red pepper

Combine all ingredients for sauce. Marinate chicken breasts, pieces or whole fryar for one hour or longer. Bake at 350 degrees for 1 hour, or whole fryar for 1 1/2 hours. Sometimes I prepare a large package of breasts, cooking two or three at a time. Will keep in marinade several days.

Hank Thompson

Gumbo

1/2 cup flour
1/2 cup oil
1 stalk celery, finely chopped
4 garlic buttons, chopped
1/4 small bottle of Kitchen Bouquet
3 pints water or broth
1 10oz. can Rotel tomatoes
2 large onions, finely chopped
1 large bell pepper, finely chopped
salt and pepper to taste
1 bay leaf
1/2 tsp. thyme
8-10 pieces of chopped okra

Make a roux by heating oil in a flat-bottomed pan, then add flour. Stir continuously until chocolate brown. Add chopped vegetables and saute. Heat liquid and add. Stir in canned tomatoes, seasoning and Kitchen Bouquet. Simmer 1 hour, do not boil.

FOR DUCK GUMBO: Use 2 to 3 ducks, parboiled, skinned and deboned. Cut into bite-sized pieces and add 45 minutes before end of cooking period.

Joe Barnhill

Joe's Homemade Bean Soup

1 bag soup mix
2 tbsp. salt
2 qts. water
2-3 ham hock or ham bone
1 large onion chopped
1 large can tomatoes
1 pod red pepper (optional)
Salt & pepper and if you like - 1 pod
    garlic

SOUP MIX: (one pound each)	
baby lima	barley
black eyed pea	split yellow pea
navy beans	green peas
lentil	black beans
red kidney	pinto beans

Place 2 cups each in baggie with recipe.

Wash beans and put in pot. Cover with water and 2 tbsp. salt and soak overnight. In the morning, drain beans, add 2 quarts water and ham hocks and simmer slowly for 2-3 hours. Add remaining ingredients and simmer 30 minutes longer. Will freeze well.

Ernie Irvan

Lemon-Garlic Grilling Sauce

1/4 cup melted butter
1/4 cup olive oil
1/4 cup lemon juice
1 tablespoon Worcestershire
  Sauce
1 tablespoon green pepper sauce
3 cloves garlic, minced

In a small bowl, combine all ingredients and blend well. Brush on seafood, poultry or vegetables during grilling. Heat any remaining sauce and serve with grilled foods.

Makes about 3/4 Cup

Sauces & Soups

Confederate Railroad

Mark Dufrense's Barbecue Sauce

6 cups of brown sugar
1/3 cup of paprika
6 tbls. salt
6 tbls. dry mustard
6 tsp. cayenne pepper
1 1/2 cups of worcestshire sauce
6 tbls. garlic salt
1/2 cup of regular mustard
8 cups of tomato juice
12 cups or 75 ozs. of tomato sauce
3 cups of ketchup
6 cups of water
1 cup Crown Royal liquor

Mix all dry spices together then add remaining spices. Simmer on low for 3 to 4 hours. Serve with chicken, beef, or pork.

Can marinate meat in vinegar for several hours.
This makes 2 1/2 gallons.

*Mark is the drummer for Confederate Railroad

Potato Soup

6-8 potatoes
1 tsp. butter
1 tsp. garlic salt
1 tsp. pepper
1 tsp. parsley

David Allen & Jodi Lynn Coe

Bring to a boil together till potatoes are cooked. Before serving, add 2 cups milk and 1/4 lb. Velveeta cheese.

David Allen Coe started his career back in the late '60's and went on stage masked. He called himself the Rhinestone Cowboy and no one knew his real name. He wanted the music to stand on its own. It wasn't until two years later, while performing with his friend, Willie Nelson, that he removed the mask.

Raw Cranberry Sauce

1 qt. cranberries
2 red Delicious apples
1/2 orange peel
2 lg. peeled oranges
1 cup honey
2 cups chopped pecans

Judy Welden

Put the cranberries, apples and orange peeling through the food chopper. Cut oranges into small sections with scissors. Add nuts to the fruit mixture and blend honey into it last. The sauce will keep well for several days in the refrigerator.

Ricky & Sharon White Skaggs

Ricky's Chicken Pickin' Corn Soup

3 or 4 chicken breasts
4 medium potatoes
2 medium onions
1 can whole kernel corn
1 can cream style corn
1 can cream of chicken soup
1 can cream of mushroom
   soup
5 tbsp. Wesson oil
1 1/2 tbsp. cornstarch
salt
pepper
McCormick's chicken
   seasoning

Cut chicken into bite-size pieces. Season with salt, pepper and chicken seasoning and brown in Wesson oil. Remove chicken from pot. Combine soups with one can water and bring to a boil. Add potatoes and onions. Add whole kernal corn and cream style corn. Bring to a boil and put chicken back in pot. Mix cornstarch with 1 cup water and add to soup, stirring well. Cover and simmer on medium heat 45 minutes to 1 hour. Stir occasionally to prevent sticking.

*Note: This is a Ricky Skaggs original that he stirred up in his own kitchen.

228

Soup Beans or Brown Beans

1-2 lb. bag dried brown beans
1-4 inch strip country bacon cut
    1" wide
1 to 2 tsp. salt

John Michael Montgomery

Wash and cook beans. Fill large pot half full of water: 4 or 6 quart preferred. Add beans.
* Bring to boil and cook on medium high heat for 15 minutes: remove from heat, drain water, run fresh water over beans: drain water, then add more fresh water return to heat on medium high. Repeat * process: after 2nd draining put beans in crock pot add hot water* country bacon cut in 1" chunks and 1 tsp salt cook on high until done, approximately 2 1/2 to 3 hours. Add 1 tsp. salt half way through cooking time if needed.

* When adding hot water in crock pot fill to 1" from top after beans are added. Add 1 large bowl and spoon, sliced onions, cornbread and Eddie, John Michael and Becky Lynn and you will have an empty crockpot.
Plates and forks can be added for individual servings: Ha, Ha!

Spaghetti Sauce

1 lb. ground beef
1/2 cup chopped onions
1 tsp. garlic salt
1- 4 oz. mushroom pies
   (optional)
1/4 cup chopped parsley or
   2 tsp. dry parsley
1- 8 oz. can tomato sauce
2 cups canned tomatoes
1 tsp. salt
1/2 tsp. oregano
1/2 tsp. pepper
1 or 2 bay leaves
dash basil
1/2 - 1 lb. dry spaghetti

Dan Truman
(Diamond Rio)

Fry beef with onions. Drain grease. Add other ingredients and simmer until dinner. Prepare pasta and serve hot. A Truman family favorite.

Serves 6. (Sauce freezes well.)

Tomato Gravy

1 1/2 cups tomatoes (1 medium
   can)
2 tbsp. oil
2 tbsp. sugar
Salt & pepper to taste
2 tbsp. flour
2 cups milk

June Carter Cash

Combine tomatoes, oil, sugar, salt and pepper in a
skillet on medium heat. Cook about 15 minutes. Mix
together the flour and milk, then add to skillet. Cook on
medium until mixture thickens. Spoon over hot
biscuits.

Nitty Gritty Dirt Band
(Jimmie Fadden, Bob Carpenter,
Jeff Hanna, Jimmy Ibbotson)

Tortilla Soup

1 dried ancho chile
1/4 cup olive oil
4 corn tortillas, cut into
    1-inch pieces
1 large onion - chopped
3 cloves garlic - minced
4 cups chicken broth
1/2 tsp. cumin
1 tbsp. chopped parsley
2 tbsp. chopped cilantro
black pepper to taste
2 tomatoes unpeeled -
    chopped

Remove stem and seeds from chile: saute in hot oil in dutch oven until soft. Remove chile, and chop, reserving drippings in dutch oven. Fry tortilla pieces in drippings until brown. Remove, drain, reserving drippings in dutch oven.

Saute onion, green pepper and garlic in drippings until tender. Add broth, cumin and pepper. Bring to a boil; reduce heat; simmer 20 minutes. Stir in reserved chile, tomatoes, simmer 10 minutes. Before serving, stir in cilantro and parsley.

To serve, place fried tortilla pieces in individual soup bowls, reserving one fourth of chips. Add soup. Top with reserved chips. (Yield: 6 cups).

Seafood

Seafood

Beer Battered Bass 235

Black Water Hattie Jambalaya 236

Brother Ray's Ceviche 237

California Crab Mold 238

Chesapeake Bay Crab Cakes 239

Crawfish Fettucini 240

Crawfish Jambalaya 241

Creole Jambalaya 242

Fried Catfish and Jalapeno Hushpuppies 243

Jeannie's Quick & Easy Salmon Patties 244

Seafood Boil 245

Shrimp and Beef Stir Fry 246

Shrimp & Crab Casserole 247

Beer Battered Bass

Tracy Byrd

5 lb. of fillets (preferably bass, but I
    guess any fish will do)
1 12 oz. beer
2 tbsp. of tabasco sauce
4 tbsp. of yellow sauce
2 packages of Corn-Kits Brand cornbread
    mix
1 cup of yellow corn meal
Salt
Pepper
1 skillet of hot grease *OR* deep fryer

1st - Mix beer, tabasco, and mustard in a large bowl
2nd - Salt and pepper the fillets and coat them with them with beer batter.
3rd - Put 1 cup of corn meal and 2 pkgs. of corn-kits in a paper grocery sack.
4th - Put battered fillets in sack and shake until fillets are thoroughly coated.
5th - Fry in grease until golden brown.

*Serve with hushpuppies, french fries, baked beans, and coleslaw, and of course a
cold beer!!!*

NOTE: To truly bring out the flavor of this recipe, you must catch the bass yourself!

Jim Stafford

Black Water Hattie Jambalaya

1 lg. onion
1 lg. bell pepper
2 pods of minced garlic
Minute Rice
2 tbsp. of bacon grease
1 small pkg. of cooked dried
   blackeyed peas
1 lb. of sausage
3 bay leaves
salt to taste
cayenne pepper to taste

Prepare blackeyed peas ahead by soaking overnight. Put blackeyed peas in large boiling pot and add cayenne pepper, garlic, salt, and a slice of salt pork. Bring blackeyed peas to a boil and simmer till tender. In a separate skillet, saute onion, bell pepper, and garlic in bacon grease. Brown sausage in this mixture. Pour off excess grease. Meanwhile prepare Minute Rice in separate pot using instructions on box. Add meat mixture, rice, and bay leaves to blackeyed peas. Season to taste and allow to simmer for 1/2 hour. Serve when ready.

Brother Ray's Ceviche

12 medium fresh shrimp
   (peeled & dried)
12 fresh sea scallops
1/2 - 1 lb. fresh redfish filets (or
   other firm fleshed fish)

THE FISH:
Be sure to use fresh fish for this recipe. If frozen fish are used, drop fish in boiling water for 1 minute and then let cool a little before marinating. The amounts may be adjusted to suit the occasion. Make enough for everybody.

Asleep At The Wheel

THE MARINADE:
Juice: 1/2 cup lemon juice (fresh squeezed), 1/4 cup lime juice (fresh squeezed)
1/4 cup orange juice (fresh squeezed), 1/8 cup tangerine juice (fresh squeezed), optional
1 tomato chopped, 1 onion chopped, 1 fresh jalapeno or serrano pepper -
   stemmed,seeded, diced (less or more or none-depending on how hot), 2 tblsp. cilantro
   chopped, a dash of tabasco (more if desired).

DIRECTIONS: Put seafood in a glass bowl, add enough of the juices to cover the seafood. Add the vegetables and cilantro. Mix gently and cover. Refrigerate at least 3 hours, but best if left overnight to marinate. Will keep refrigerated for 3 days. Serve in individual glasses or on a plate on a bed of lettuce with a couple slices of avocado, corn chips, sprig of cilantro and lemon, lime or orange slices as a garnish.

R.W. Smith
(The California Cowboys)

California Crab Mold

1- 6 oz. or 8 oz. of cream cheese
2 green onions, chopped fine
1 can cream of mushroom soup
1 pkg. of knox gelatine -
    dissolved in 3 tbsp. of cold
    water
7 oz. crab (can or fresh)
1 cup chopped celery
1 cup mayonnaise

Heat soup on low fire. Dissolve gelatine and add to warm soup.
Cool slightly and mix remaining ingredients to soup mixture.
Add to mold and chill overnight. Serve with favorite crackers.

This is a favorite recipe that we serve every Christmas.
This is my Gramma Hilda's famous recipe . . .

Jamie McMurray

Chesapeake Bay Crab Cakes

1/2 lb. fresh crab meat
1/2 green pepper (chopped)
1 small red onion (chopped)
1 small white onion (chopped)
1 tsp. vegetable salt
1/2 tsp. pepper
1/2 tsp. fresh chopped parsley
1 cup bread crumbs
1 cup cornbread crumbs
2 eggs (well beaten)
1/4 cup heavy cream
1/8 cup melted butter

Pre-cook onions and green peppers, taking care not to loose firmness. Mix crab meat, beaten eggs, the onions and green pepper, vegetable salt, parsley, bread crumbs and cream. Toss lightly, mixing well. In heavy skillet add melted butter, pre-cook until brown, do not burn. Remove from heat and add hand molded crab cake mixture, no more than 1/2 to 3/4 inches thick. Return to heat, low to medium. When brown on sides, turn and cook 1 1/2 to 2 minutes, do not over cook. Remove at once from skillet, do not let soak up butter.

Remember not to add salt, crab meat contains the delicate flavors from the salty sea.

Doug Kershaw

Crawfish Fettucini

3 sticks butter
3 med. chopped onions
3 ribs vhopped celery
1/4 cup flour
2 chopped bell peppers
3 lbs. crawfish or shrimp
2 pints half and half cream
1 16oz. package Velveeta Cheese - cubed
1 16oz. package. fettucini noodles
1 can Rotel tomatoes (diced)
salt and pepper to taste

Saute onions, bell pepper and celery in butter. When limp add Rotel, flour and mix well. Cover and cook 5 minutes on low. Stir occasionally. Add crawfish or shrimp, cook 20 minutes stirring often. Add cream, cheese, salt and pepper, mix well. Cook on low 20 minutes. Cook noodles, drain, add to sauce. Serve.

This recipe is from my sister-in-law, Marie Kershaw. It can also be make using more low-calorie ingredients. Bon appetit!

Crawfish Jambalaya

1 lb. peeled crawfish tails
1 can (14.5 oz.) beef broth
1 can (8 oz.) tomato sauce
1 jar (8 oz.) drained mushrooms, finely chopped
1 medium onion, finely chopped
1 bell pepper, finely chopped
1 jalepeno pepper, finely chopped
1/2 cup of fresh parsley, finely chopped
1 stick butter
*2 1/2 cups of raw long-grain rice, white Tony Chachere's creole seasoning to taste-additional dash of salt if desired

Lana Anderson

*NOTE: use measuring cup from rice cooker to measure rice.
You will need an 8-10 cup electric rice cooker-(Hitachi)

Mix all ingredients, except butter, in a large bowl. Place the butter in the rice cooker liner and put in a heated oven to melt (butter will burn easily; watch closely). Remove liner from the oven and place all other ingredients in the cooker. Turn cooker on full setting (usually about 25-30 minutes) and DO NOT RAISE LID WHILE COOKING. When the bell on the cooker rings, cook JAMBALAYA an additional 30 minutes longer on warm. DO NOT RAISE LID, this will cause the moisture and steam to leave the cooker. Will serve 6-8. Great served with a tossed salad and hot bread.

Dinah Shore

(*In Memory*)

1 cup frozen or cooked lobster tails, cut in
    small pieces
1 cup crab meat (optional)
1 1/3 cups cooked chicken, diced
2 Italian sausages, cut into slices and fried
    until well done

Creole Jambalaya

2 tbls. butter (heaping)
1 tbls. oil
2 onions, chopped
1 clove garlic, chopped
1 slice lean ham, cubed (approximately
    1/2 cup)
3 tomatoes, chopped
1/2 cup tomato juice or 1 8-oz. can
    tomato sauce
salt and pepper to taste
pinch thyme
dash of chili pepper
1 bay leaf
4 oz. sherry
4 cups chicken broth
1 cup rice
1 cup raw shrimp, cleaned

In large pot, saute garlic and onions in butter and oil. Add ham. When onions are brown and ham is slightly browned, add tomatoes and tomato juice or sauce. Add bay leaf and season generously with salt, pepper, thyme and chili pepper. Simmer for ten minutes. Then add chicken broth. When mixture starts boiling, add rice. After rice has cooked about fifteen minutes, add sausages, shrimp (deveined) and lobster tails, cut in small pieces. Add chicken and crab meat at the last minute. Stir frequently until rice is tender. Add a wine glass of sherry. Cook five minutes longer and remove from heat. Serve with crusty warm French sour dough bread, Brie cheese and a light salad. Serves eight to ten. (From *Someone's In The Kitchen With Dinah*)

Fried Catfish and Jalapeno Hushpuppies

Tracy Lawrence

10 whole medium sized catfish
  (cleaned)
1 lb. corn meal (yellow)
1 jar grey poupon mustard
salt and pepper
1 lg. onion (chopped)
6 jalapeno peppers (chopped)
1 1/2 cups buttermilk

Fill deep fryer with cooking oil. Heat until Hot! Coat each fish with salt, pepper and mustard. Roll in cornmeal. Place fish in hot oil. When fish rises back to top of oil, it should be done. Remove and drain on paper towel!

HUSHPUPPIES
Mix corn meal, salt, pepper, onion, jalapeno pepper and buttermilk. Roll into medium balls. Drop into hot oil. Cook until golden brown. Serve with catfish!

Jeannie's Quick & Easy Salmon Patties

Jeannie C. Riley

1 egg
1/2 cup flour
1 1/2 tsp. baking powder
1 lg. can pink salmon
1/3 cup onion
3/4 cup Crisco

Drain salmon, set aside 2 tbsp. of the juice in a medium mixing bowl. Mix salmon, egg and onion until sticky. Stir in flour. Add baking powder to salmon mixture. Form into small patties and fry until golden brown in the hot 3/4 cup Crisco (about 5 minutes). Serve with tartar sauce or caesar salad dressing.

Serves 4 to 6.

Jeannie was born Oct 19th in Anson, Texas (Jones County). Her daughter, Kim Riley Coyle is also a talented singer and has sung backup for her mother for several years.

Seafood Boil

Eddy Raven

8 red potatoes
8 small pieces of corn on the cob
2 lbs. of sausage
3 lbs. of shrimp
4 lbs. of crab legs
1 dozen clams (in shell)
2 crab boil bags

Fill 10 to 15 quart pot 1/4 full of water and bring to a boil. Place boil bags and plenty of seasoning into water. Add the potatoes and let cook for 10 minutes, then add the sausage and let cook 5 minutes. Next add the corn and all the seafood and cook until done (about 10 minutes).

It's easy, all you do is throw it in and let it boil!

Jeff Cook
(Alabama)

Shrimp and Beef Stir Fry

cubed beef
deveined shrimp
red and green peppers
zucchini squash
white onions
soy sauce
ground ginger
Coca Cola

Start cubed beef in hot wok stirring until seared on all sides. Add peeled and deveined shrimp, sliced red and green peppers. zucchini squash, and white onions. Season with soy sauce and ground ginger. Dilute soy sauce with Coca Cola and stir two or three minutes or just until vegetables are tender crisp. Serve over rice.

Shrimp & Crab Casserole

4 tbsp. flour
1/3 tsp. salt
1/3 tsp. pepper
2 cup milk
1/3 cup Cheese Whiz
1 cup grated cheese
1/8 tsp. tabasco
1/2 lb. cooked shrimp
1/4 lb. crabmeat

Ned Jarrett

Mix flour, salt & pepper with part of milk (1/4 c.). Beat all lumps out. Add Cheese Whiz to rest of milk in double boiler. When Cheese Whiz has melted, add flour mixture and tabasco. Stir until smooth and thickened. Add shrimp and crabmeat. Pour into casserole and top with grated cheese. Bake at 350 degrees for 20 minutes.

After driving in NASCAR racing for 13 years, and winning 50 NASCAR Winston Cup Races, Ned has retired to a wonderful career in broadcasting. He and his wife, Martha, have two sons , Glenn and Dale, and one daughter Patti J. Makar. Dale has become a prominent NASCAR driver in his own right.

Notes

Vegetables

Vegetables

Baked Beans 251
Cabbage Rolls 252
Christy's Festive Baked Beans 253
Fried Corn.. 254
Gourmet Potatoes 255
Greek Spinach & Rice 256
Hearty Eggplant-Barley Saute 257
Potato Casserole 258
Richard's Roasted Peppers 259
Stuffed Green Peppers.. 260
Stuffed Potatoes 261

Vegetables

Baked Beans

1 lb. ground beef
2 cans pork & beans
1 cup brown sugar
1/2 cup catsup
1/2 cup Coca-Cola
1 small onion - diced
2 teaspoons dry mustard
sliced bacon - diced

Billy Standridge

Brown ground beef and drain. Mix beans, brown sugar, catsup, coca cola, onion, mustard & beef and place in a 13x9 casserole dish. Dot top with bacon. Bake at 300 degrees, uncovered, for 1 1/2 to 2 hours.

Delicious

Michelle Wright

Cabbage Rolls

2 lbs. lean ground beef
2-3 cups of cooked unrinsed rice
2 slices of bacon (finely chopped)
1 large onion (finely chopped)
2 stalks of celery (finely chopped)
1 large head of cabbage
salt, pepper, garlic powder &
   seasoning spices to taste
tomato, clamato, V-8 juice or similar agent

Cook rice. Brown beef, onion and bacon together. Drain fat and add spices. Combine cooked rice (unrinsed) to beef mixture, checking spices to taste.

Wash and separate cabbage leaves. Roll about two large tbsp. of meat and rice mixture into leaf. Do this continually until all meat and rice mixture is used.

Spray bottom of baking pan with Pam, or similar agent. Place rolls in baking or roasting pan no more than three layers high. Pour one or a combination of juices over the rolls ensuring that all are covered with liquid. Check and/or baste rolls with juice during cooking time. You may want to cover rolls with any leftover cabbage leaves to protect from burning. Best when cooked (covered) 4-5 hours in a slow oven at 275 degrees F.

Vegetables

Christy's Festive Baked Beans

1 can Big John's Bean's & Fixin's
1 tsp. grey poupon dijon mustard
1/2 cup onion, diced
1/2 cup green pepper, diced
1/2 jar mushrooms, diced
1 small carrot, diced
1 tbsp. catsup
2 tbsp. brown sugar
1 tbsp. sherry cooking wine
1 clove minced garlic

Christy Lane

In baking dish mix beans & fixin's and all ingredients listed. Top with slices of bacon or ham (fat trimmed off). Bake in 350 degree oven for 45 minutes or until done.

John Michael Montgomery

Vegetables

Fried Corn

5 cups of fresh corn cut off cob
   (Silver Queen if available)
1 stick of margarine
3 tbsp. of country or jowl bacon
   drippings
1 tsp. of salt
1 tbsp. of sugar
1/4 tsp. pepper (if desired)
1 to 2 cups water
1 tbsp. self-rising flour

Melt margarine in 8 or 10 inch iron skillet, add bacon drippings reserving 1 tbsp. Stir fresh corn into medium hot skillet, add 1 cup of water and all other ingredients except 1 tbsp. bacon drippings. Cook on medium to medium high heat, stirring often. Cover and cook liquid down and then add second cup of water. Cook liquid down again. Turn burner down to medium low: stir 1 tbsp. bacon drippings into flour, blend thoroughly: stir into skillet of corn. Stir constantly to prevent scorching. Remove from heat when corn has thickened. Pour in a bowl, add a big spoon and hungry people. A plate and fork can be used if desired.

Vegetables

Gourmet Potatoes

6-8 lg. potatoes
1 1/2 cup sour cream
2 cup cheddar cheese, grated
1/2 cup butter
1/2 cup salad dressing
1/2 cup onions, grated
olives or ham (optional)

Vince Gill

Bake potatoes, then slice into round pieces. Grease dish.
Place potato slices in dish. Then layer other items as
listed: sour cream, cheese, butter, salad dressing, onions,
optional items. Bake at 350 degrees until brown.

Greek Spinach & Rice

2-3 tbls. olive oil
1 lg. onion
1 pkg. or bunch fresh spinach,
    washed & drained. (stems on)
1- 8 oz. can tomato sauce
1 1/2 cups water
heaping 1/2 cup Uncle Ben's
    regular rice (or brown rice)
Vege-Sal or salt, & pepper to taste

Lane Brody

In large pot, saute onion in oil until soft. Then add the remaining ingredients. Cover and cook, stirring occasionally. Continue simmering until rice is done.

Serve with fresh-squeezed lemon, or parmesan cheese, or Louisiana Hot Sauce or plain. However you prefer.

Vegetables

Hearty Eggplant-Barley Saute

1/2 cup chopped onion

1/2 cup chopped mushrooms

1/4 cup chopped green pepper

1 tbsp. minced garlic

1 tsp. olive oil

1 cup cubed eggplant

1 can (16 oz) chopped tomatoes

3/4 cup quick-cooking barley

1/2 cup chili sauce

1/4 cup snipped freshed parsley

1 tsp. honey

1 tsp. Worcestershire sauce

1/2 tsp. dried Marjoram

1/4 tsp. black pepper

Nitty Gritty Dirt Band
(Jimmie Fadden, Bob Carpenter, Jeff Hanna, Jimmy Ibbotson)

In large non-stick skillet, over medium heat, saute the onions, mushrooms, pepper and garlic in the oil until softened, about 5 minutes. Add the eggplant and 2 tbsp. water; saute until softened, about 10 minutes.

Add the tomatoes, 1 1/2 cups water, barley, chili sauce, parsley, honey, Worcestershire sauce, Marjoram and black pepper. Bring to a boil, then reduce heat and simmer until barley is tender, about 20 minutes. Serves four.

257

Vegetables

Potato Casserole

2 lbs frozen hashbrowns,
    thawed
1/2 cup melted butter
1/4 to 1/2 tsp. salt
1/2 Cup chopped onion
1 pint sour cream
1 can cream of chicken
    soup
2 Cups grated cheddar
    cheese

The Statler Brothers
*(Johnny Fortune, Harold Reid,
Don Reid, Phil Balsley)*

Topping:
2 Cups crushed corn flakes
1/4 cup melted butter

Mix all, except topping. Bake in greased 9"x15" glass dish 350° for
25 to 30 minutes. Until bubbly and brown.
Put topping on during last 10 minutes.

Vegetables

Richard's Roasted Peppers

1 large can of roasted red peppers
2 large cloves of garlic
2 tblsp oregano
2 tblsp basil
1/2 tsp rosemary
1 tblsp black pepper
1/2 cup extra virgin olive oil
salt

Richard and Donna Sterban
(The Oak Ridge Boys)

You will need a medium sized rectangular dish with a cover. Pour peppers, olive oil, and other ingredients in to dish. Mix thoroughly so that all peppers are coated. Refrigerate for at least 24 hours. Serve in a salad or alone with warm Italian bread.

Richard Petty

Vegetables

Stuffed Green Peppers

1 1/2 lb. ground beef
1 medium onion, chopped fine
1 tbsp. chili powder
2 eggs
1 cup catsup
1 cup cornflakes
6 bell peppers cut in half and
   cleaned
Salt and pepper to taste

Boil peppers 5 minutes. Mix other ingredients together. Stuff peppers with mixture and arrange in bottom of large pyrex dish.

Sauce
2 1/2 cups catsup & tomato paste, use more catsup than paste
2 tbsp. ground mustard
1 tbsp. vinegar
2 tbsp. brown sugar
Mix well and pour over peppers. Bake at 375 degrees, 30 to 40 minutes.

Vegetables

Stuffed Potatoes

2 large baking potatoes
1/4 cups sour cream (reduced fat)
2 tbsp. minced chives
2 tbsp. grated fresh parmesan
   cheese
1 tbsp. 2% milk
1/2 tsp. salt
1/8 tsp. garlic powder
pepper
paprika

Kim Forester
(Forester Sisters)

Wash potatoes and bake at 375° for 1 hour or until done. Let cool. Cut potatoes in half lengthwise. Scoop out pulp, leaving 1/4 inch shell. Set shells aside. Combine pulp, sour cream, chives, cheese, milk, salt, garlic and pepper in a medium bowl. Mash until fluffy. Spoon mixture into shells an place onto baking sheet. Sprinkle with paprika and bake, uncovered, 10 minutes or until heated through.

Notes

_____

_____

_____

_____

_____

_____

_____

_____

_____

_____

_____

_____

_____

Index

A

Aaron Tippin - 100
Alabama - 14, 49, 197, 246
Alan Jackson - 48
Alice Detrick - 73
Allison Jordan - 86
Amanda Thomas - 3
Amy Grant - 126
Asleep At The Wheel - 237

B

B.J. Thomas - 117
Barbara Fairchild - 53
Barbara Mandrell - 62, 204
Bellamy Brothers - 26, 105
Bill & Gail Davis - 115, 221
Bill Anderson - 203
Bill Elliott - 149
Billy Ray Cyrus - 171
Billy Standridge - 251
Billy Thomas - 194
Blaise Alexander - 22, 153
Bob Carpenter - 232, 257
Brother Phelps - 29
Brooks & Dunn - 141, 142
Buck Owens - 119
Buckshot Jones - 114, 177

C

Carter Family - 123
Charlie Chase - 113
Charlie Daniels - 47, 57, 97
Chris Hussey - 77, 122
Christy Forester - 21, 34
Christy Lane - 253
Cissie Lynn - 15
Confederate Railroad - 225
Crook & Chase - 113, 183
Crystal Gayle - 39

D

Dan Truman - 230
Dana Williams - 155
Darrell Waltrip - 125
Darryl Wayne - 144
David Allen & Jodi Lynn Coe - 226
David Bellamy - 26, 105
Debbie Gibson - 195
Derrick Gilchrist - 124
Diamond Rio - 52, 131, 155, 210, 230
Dinah Shore - 242
Dolly Parton - 109, 163
Don Reid - 56, 79, 175, 258
Donna Fargo - 33
Donnie Allison - 40
Doug Phelps - 29
Doug Kershaw - 240
Doug Stone - 187
Doug Supernaw - 54
Duane & Norah Lee Allen - 69
Duane West - 110
Duncan Cameron - 170

E

Eddy Raven - 245
Emmylou Harris - 74
Ernie Irvan - 224

F

Faith Hill - 138
Forester Sisters -
   21, 34, 150, 165, 215, 216, 261

G

Gene Johnson - 131
George Jones - 178
Glen Campbell - 96
Gogi Grant - 205, 208
Gordon Stoker - 110

Celebrity Chefs of Country Music & Motorsports

Grandpa Jones - 25
Gregg Hubbard - 170

H

Hal Ketchem - 80
Hank Thompson - 36, 140, 148, 222
Hank Williams, Jr. - 91
Harold Reid - 56, 79, 175, 258
Highway 101 - 206
Howard Bellamy - 26, 105
Hut Stricklin - 67, 164

I

Irlene Mandrell - 139

J

Jaine Fricke - 78
Jamie McMurray - 239
Janis Gill - 181
Jeannie C. Riley - 244
Jeff Burton - 121
Jeff Cook - 246
Jeff Hanna - 232, 257
Jennifer McCarter - 169
Jim Scholten - 170
Jim Stafford - 236
Jimmie Fadden - 232, 257
Jimmy Ibbotson - 232, 257
Jimmy O - 52
Jody Lynn - 135
Joe and Mary Bonsall - 20
Joe Barnhill - 223
Joe Diffie - 59
Joe Nemechek - 98
Joe Smyth - 170
John Andretti - 44
John Michael Montgomery - 156, 168, 229, 254
Johnny Benson - 158
Johnny Cash - 103
Johnny Fortune - 56, 79, 175, 258
Johnny Rodriguez - 35
Johnny Rutherford - 75
Judy Welden - 227
June Carter Cash - 231
June Forester - 165

K

Kathy Forester - 215, 216
Kathy Mattea - 76
Ken Schrader - 71
Kenny Irwin, Jr. - 116
Kenny Rogers - 207
Kevin LaPage - 179
Kim Forester - 150, 261
Kix Brooks - 142
Kristine Arnold - 181

L

Lacy J. Dalton - 120
Lana Anderson - 241
Lane Brody - 256
Larry & Margaret Fuda - 19, 81
Larry Stewart - 51
Leroy Van Dyke - 28
Linda Ronstadt - 27
Lisa Stewart - 219
Loretta Lynn - 196
Lorianne Crook - 183
Lorrie Morgan - 4, 85
Louise Mandrell - 66
Loy Allen Jr. - 186

M

Mario Gosselin - 118
Mark Collie - 159
Mark DuFresne - 225
Mark Green - 102
Mark Herndon - 197
Mark Martin - 193
Mark Miller - 170
Mark Olson - 104
Mark Smith - 46, 188
Marty Roe - 210
Marty Stuart - 8
McBride & The Ride - 72, 194
McCarter Sisters - 169, 198
Megan Sheehan - 82, 83, 211
Mel Tillis - 136
Merle Haggard - 32, 60, 214
Michael Waltrip - 5, 11
Michelle Wright - 160, 252

Mickey Gilley - 134
Mike Dillon - 180
Mike Skinner - 192
Mila Mason - 157

N

Naomi Judd - 12, 50
Neal Matthews - 110
Ned Jarrett - 247
Nikki Nelson - 206
Nitty Gritty Dirt Band - 232, 257

P

Pat Seavers - 145
Patty Loveless - 167, 212
Paul Overstreet - 10
Penny Gilley - 199
Peter Sospenzo - 209
Phil Balsley - 56, 79, 175, 258
Pirates of the Mississippi - 145

R

R.W. Smith - 238
Ralph Ezell - 13
Randy LaJoie - 166
Randy Owen - 49
Randy Travis - 37
Ray Herndon - 72
Ray Stevens - 87
Ray Walker - 110
Reba McEntire - 127
Red Steagall - 112
Richard and Donna Sterban - 259
Richard Petty - 43, 260
Rick Mast - 176
Ricky Lee Phelps - 29
Ricky Skaggs - 45, 228
Ricky Van Shelton - 132
Ronnie Dunn - 141
Ronnie McDowell - 58, 70
Ronnie Reeves - 89
Ryan Newman - 23

S

Sawyer Brown - 170

Celebrity Chefs of Country Music & Motorsports

Shelby Lynne - 24
Shenandoah - 13
Sterling Marlin - 147
Steve Wariner - 184
Suzy Bogguss - 190
Sweethearts of the Rodeo - 181

T

Tanya Tucker - 38, 99, 220
Ted Musgrave - 65
Teddy Gentry - 14
Teresa McCarter - 198
The California Cowboys - 238
The Jayhawks - 104
The Jordanaires - 110
The Oak Ridge Boys - 20, 69, 84, 259
The Statler Brothers - 56, 79, 175, 258
Tom T. Hall - 106
Tony Stewart - 133
Trace Burton - 189
Tracy Byrd - 235
Tracy Lawrence - 243
Tracy Lynne - 31
Travis Tritt - 101
Trisha Yearwood - 9, 111
Troy Beebe - 6, 61, 88, 143, 191
Ty Herndon - 90

V

Vern Gosdin - 213
Vikki Carr - 95
Vince Gill - 255

W

Ward Burton - 7, 30, 68, 154
William Lee and Brenda Golden - 84
Willie Nelson - 182
Wynonna Judd - 137

Celebrity Chefs of Country Music & Motorsports

Lehi Christian Children's Foundation

817 Connecticut Avenue • Roanoke, VA 24012 • 1-800-861-7355

ORDER FORM

Please send _____ copies of the *Celebrity Chefs of Country Music and Motorsports* cookbook.

Payment Method:

☐ Money Order ☐ Check

☐ Credit Card
☐ VISA ☐ MasterCard ☐ DISCOVER ☐ ⬤

$27.95(U.S.) or $39.95(Canada) x _____ books = $ _____

$5.95* S/H for first book = $ ____ *5.95*

*For orders outside the continental United States or multiple books, call for shipping fee

Subtotal = $ _____

Exp. Date:_____

Card No.:_____

VA residents add 4.5% sales tax (Subtotal x 0.045) = $ _____

TOTAL = $ _____

Signature:_____

Name:_____ Ph:(_____)_____

Street:_____

City:_____ St:_____ Zip:_____

Please allow 4 to 6 weeks for delivery

✂ -

Lehi Christian Children's Foundation

817 Connecticut Avenue • Roanoke, VA 24012 • 1-800-861-7355

ORDER FORM

Please send _____ copies of the *Celebrity Chefs of Country Music and Motorsports* cookbook.

Payment Method:

☐ Money Order ☐ Check

☐ Credit Card
☐ VISA ☐ MasterCard ☐ DISCOVER ☐ ⬤

$27.95(U.S.) or $39.95(Canada) x _____ books = $ _____

$5.95* S/H for first book = $ ____ *5.95*

*For orders outside the continental United States or multiple books, call for shipping fee

Subtotal = $ _____

Exp. Date:_____

Card No.:_____

VA residents add 4.5% sales tax (Subtotal x 0.045) = $ _____

TOTAL = $ _____

Signature:_____

Name:_____ Ph:(_____)_____

Street:_____

City:_____ St:_____ Zip:_____

Please allow 4 to 6 weeks for delivery

✂ -

You may also order online at: *www.celebritychefs.org*